E.A.C.H.
Little Step

E.A.C.H.
Little Step
365-Day Affirmation Journal
for Preemie Moms

Dr. Launice Melbourne

purposely
created
PUBLISHING

EACH LITTLE STEP
Published by Purposely Created Publishing Group™
Copyright © 2017 Launice Melbourne

All rights reserved.

Printed in the United States of America
ISBN: 978-1-947054-15-8

Special discounts are available on bulk quantity purchases by book clubs, associations and special interest groups. For details email: sales@publishyourgift.com or call (888) 949-6228.

For information logon to:
www.PublishYourGift.com

Dedication

To all the amazing Mothers who fight with blood, sweat, and tears through the NICU journey to see their preemies succeed, this is for all of you.

Table of Contents

My Story

As a woman who hopes to one day be a mom, I have a very special place in my heart for mothers. Through my work with preemies, I have close contact with preemie moms. I have watched them deal with feelings of guilt and sadness. I have watched them try to understand the complex issues their preemies face, and I have seen them become overwhelmed. It was in these moments that I found myself wishing I could do more to connect with and help these moms. These preemie stories I've witnessed have inspired this affirmation journal to encourage and support moms on their NICU journeys with their preemies.

Introduction

The journey through the Neonatal Intensive Care Unit ("NICU") with a preemie can often be a challenging one. It may feel lonely and be filled with an up-and-down roller coaster of emotions. It is a unique path that some mothers and their preemies must take. Despite these difficulties, every mom has the choice to be positive and see the good in the situation. This *EACH LITTLE STEP* affirmation journal is especially designed for preemie moms because "Every Amazing Child Hopes!" It is designed to help moms reflect on their journey through the NICU and beyond, and the amazing things that their preemies are doing every day to make it home. As you take the time to go through this journal day-by-day, remember that hope is one of the greatest gifts we have in the world!

Delivery
Affirmations

PRE-DELIVERY

Within me is a tower of strength
and I will survive.

REFLECTION: What is one thing you can
do today to build up your strength?

....

....

....

....

....

....

....

....

....

....

....

I breathe in calmness, and breathe out
stress and anxiety. I am at peace.

REFLECTION: Write down a time each day
when you can take a moment to meditate
or think about something positive.

....

....

....

....

....

....

....

....

....

....

I accept that I cannot control this situation, but I can control how I respond.

REFLECTION: Write down one positive way you can respond to whatever you are facing today.

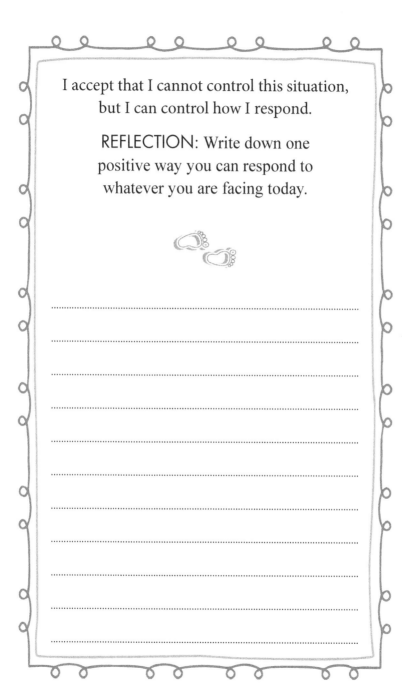

....

....

....

....

....

....

....

....

....

....

....

Every day inside my womb my baby
grows bigger and stronger!

REFLECTION: Write down how
many days you have been
able to avoid delivery.

....

....

....

....

....

....

....

....

....

....

....

Today I am at peace and I remain
calm as my contractions lessen.

REFLECTION: What song helps
you to relax? Play that song now
and focus on remaining calm.

....

....

....

....

....

....

....

....

....

....

Getting admitted to the hospital is not what I expected but I am always up for a challenge!

REFLECTION: Write down one person who has made this experience easier for you so far.

....

....

....

....

....

....

....

....

....

....

Hearing all about an early delivering was overwhelming but I have hope!

REFLECTION: Write down what you are feeling at this very moment. How can you reshape your thoughts to focus on something hopeful?

....

....

....

....

....

....

....

....

....

....

I let go of the plan I thought I had for delivery, and work with my medical team for a new plan.

REFLECTION: Embrace the new plan and write it down.

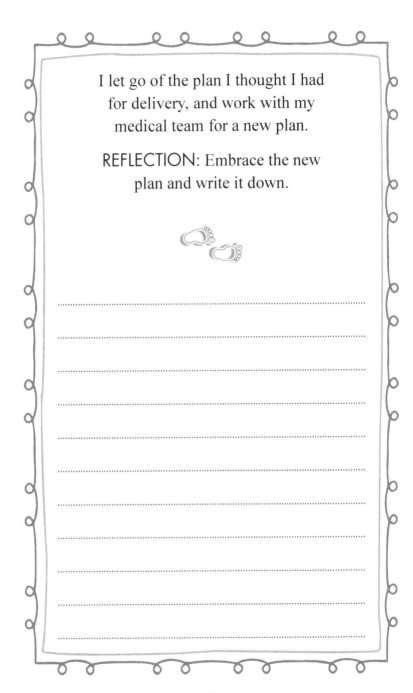

....

....

....

....

....

....

....

....

....

....

....

I mourn the loss of a typical pregnancy and
delivery, and I focus on the path ahead.

REFLECTION: What advice would
you give to help a mother who may
have to face a similar situation?

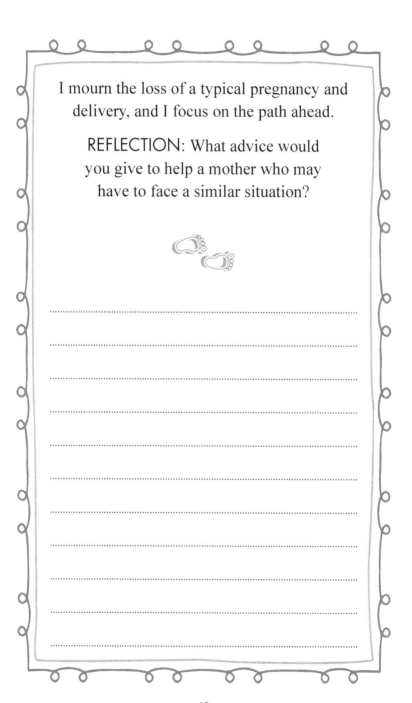

....

....

....

....

....

....

....

....

....

....

I am at the start of a daunting
but incredible journey!

REFLECTION: Think about one thing you
know right now you and your baby will
need for this journey. Write it down.

....

....

....

....

....

....

....

....

....

....

....

....

....

....

....

....

I know my body can handle
whatever is about to happen.

REFLECTION: Write down three
ways you prepared for pregnancy.

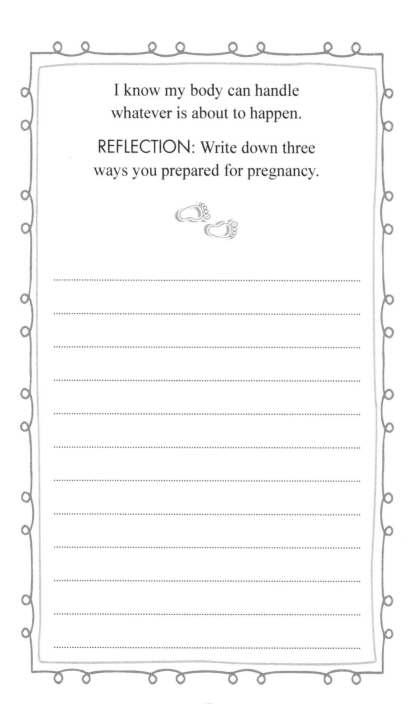

....

....

....

....

....

....

....

....

....

....

....

....

Everyone may not understand my
decisions for this baby, but I am
doing what is best for my family.

REFLECTION: Write down your greatest
wish right now for your preemie.

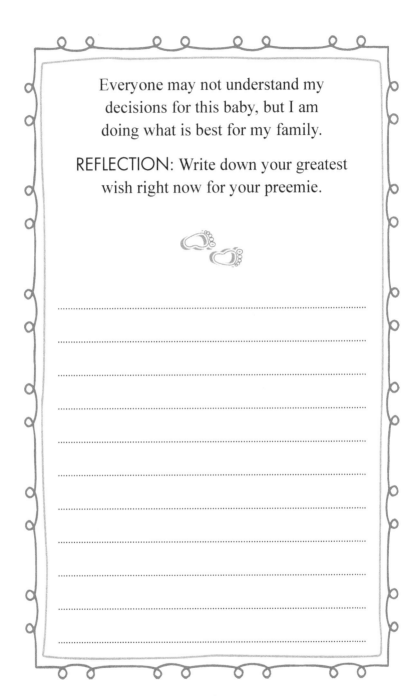

....

....

....

....

....

....

....

....

....

....

As I go into labor, I will remain calm
and trust that all will be well.

REFLECTION: Who will be
at your side to help you through
this delivery?

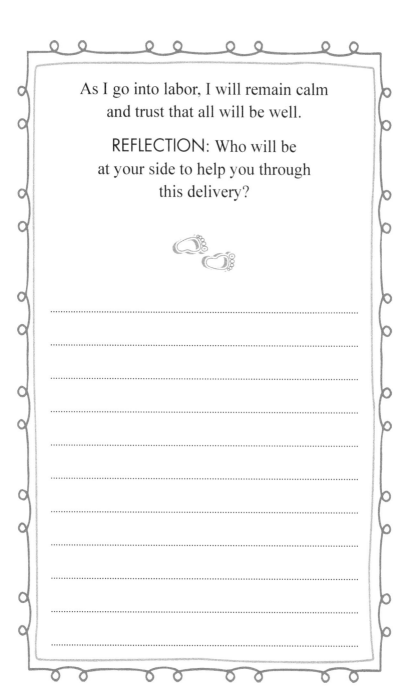

....

....

....

....

....

....

....

....

....

....

My baby is in sync with me
at all times.

REFLECTION: How do you feel
right now? What can you do to
remain peaceful and serene?

....

....

....

....

....

....

....

....

....

....

I'm blocking out everything.
I will focus and work on breathing so
I can help deliver my baby safely.

REFLECTION: As you focus inward,
what is your body telling you?

....

....

....

....

....

....

....

....

....

....

I am at one with my body.
I feel my baby moving,
and I know that my baby is okay.

REFLECTION: What else helps you
feel in tune with your baby?

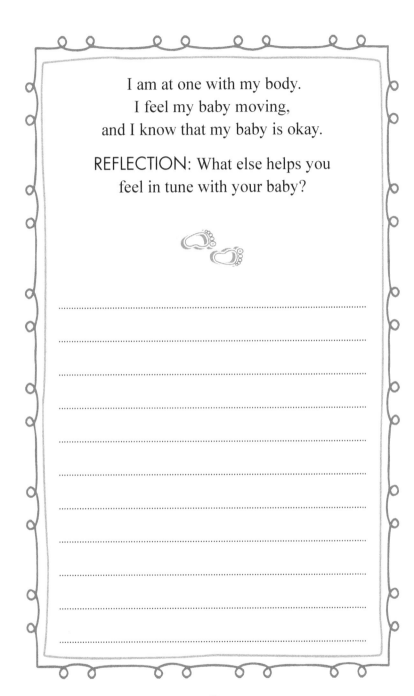

....

....

....

....

....

....

....

....

....

I am able to handle the pain
I am feeling now because I know
it will not last forever.

REFLECTION: Repeat to yourself over
and over, "This will not last forever."

....

....

....

....

....

....

....

....

....

I trust that the doctors
are doing their very best for
my preemie and me.

REFLECTION: Write down who
is a part of your O.B. team.

....

....

....

....

....

....

....

....

....

....

....

Delivery Affirmations

POST-DELIVERY

All of the intense pain was worth
it just to see my baby's face!

REFLECTION: What was the
hardest part of your delivery?
How did you overcome it?

....

....

....

....

....

....

....

....

....

....

My baby made it through
delivery and I am grateful!

REFLECTION: Name one other thing
that you are grateful for today.

Delivery was tough, but I made it through!

REFLECTION: Recall another time in your life when you made it through something difficult. Write it down.

....

....

....

....

....

....

....

....

....

....

....

After several months of waiting to
meet my baby, s/he is finally here.

REFLECTION: Describe
how it felt to meet your baby
for the first time.

....

....

....

....

....

....

....

....

....

....

....

....

My baby is a wonderful expression of love.

REFLECTION: Write down three ways in which you show your love to others.

....

....

....

....

....

....

....

....

....

....

....

Seeing my baby's face for the
first time changed my life.

REFLECTION: What do you remember
most about this moment?

....

....

....

....

....

....

....

....

....

....

....

....

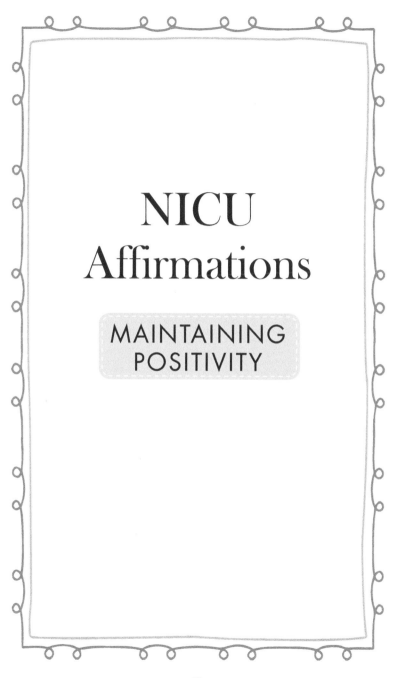

NICU
Affirmations

MAINTAINING
POSITIVITY

Today begins a new chapter
of my life as a mother.

REFLECTION: Write down
how you know you are ready.

....

....

....

....

....

....

....

....

....

....

My baby made it through her/his
first day in life and I am blessed.

REFLECTION: Write down one thing
you want to tell your baby about this
moment when s/he is all grown up.

....

....

....

....

....

....

....

....

....

....

....

I protected my baby while on the inside, and I will do whatever I can to protect my baby on the outside!

REFLECTION: Write down your plan for how you will protect your baby right now.

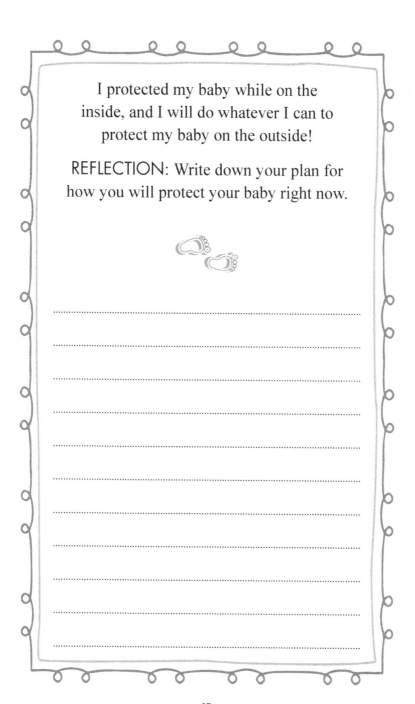

....

....

....

....

....

....

....

....

....

....

My dream to be a mother has been fulfilled!

REFLECTION: This may not
have been how you imagined your
baby's delivery, but how has this
process been a blessing so far?

....

....

....

....

....

....

....

....

....

....

My baby is so small, but I
know s/he can make it!

REFLECTION: Your baby has made it
through the first hurdle: delivery. Take time
to reflect on this moment and be thankful.

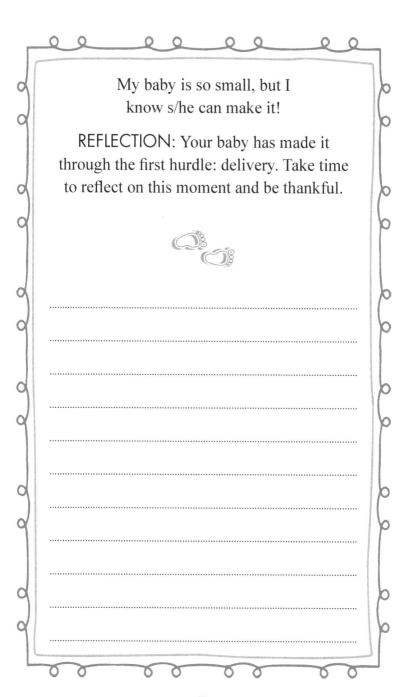

....

....

....

....

....

....

....

....

....

....

I pray for blessings for my preemie
from the crown of her/his head
down to her/his little toes.

REFLECTION: What blessings has
your preemie received thus far?

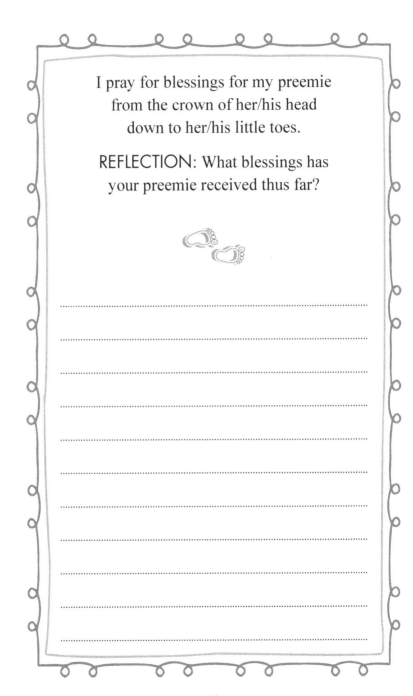

....

....

....

....

....

....

....

....

....

....

....

Today and everyday
I am filled with so much love;
it overflows into everything I do.

REFLECTION: Write down five people
you love. Call them today and tell them.

....

....

....

....

....

....

....

....

....

....

I have a family that loves and
supports my preemie and me.

REFLECTION: Who in your family are
you most excited for your baby to meet?

....

....

....

....

....

....

....

....

....

....

....

....

The journey ahead seems long but I'm ready!

REFLECTION: What is the next big goal
your baby will reach? Write it down.

....

....

....

....

....

....

....

....

....

....

God called me to be a mother! I
am a mother and this is one of the
greatest gifts in the world!

REFLECTION: What's your
mom superpower?

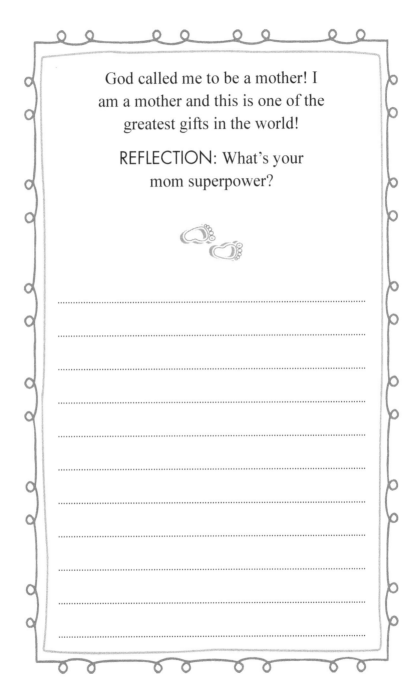

....

....

....

....

....

....

....

....

....

....

Today my baby opened her/his eyes.

REFLECTION: Describe how
that made you feel.

....

....

....

....

....

....

....

....

....

....

....

....

It's hard to be at my baby's bedside and not be able to touch or hold her/him, but I have faith s/he feels my presence and knows I'm here.

REFLECTION: Have you placed pictures of yourself in your baby's room? If not, put up a picture so that you are always there.

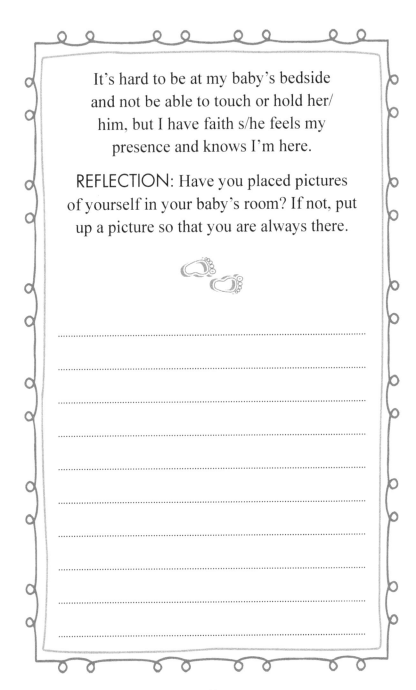

....

....

....

....

....

....

....

....

....

There are all these unfamiliar faces
in my baby's room but they are
helping keep my baby safe.

REFLECTION: Write down who
is taking care of your baby.

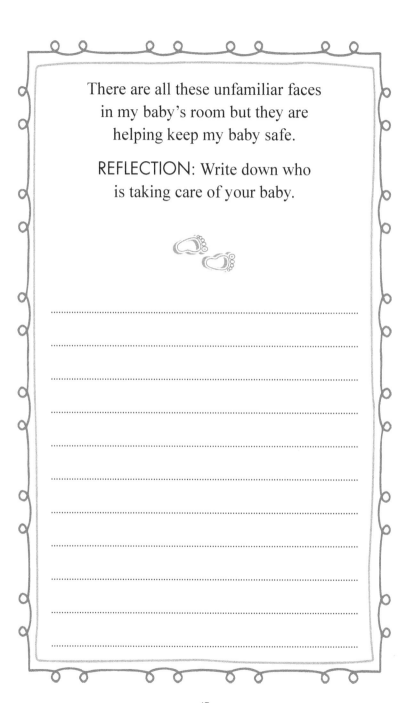

....

....

....

....

....

....

....

....

....

....

I believe in my preemie!

REFLECTION: Write down how long
your preemie has been in the NICU.
What has been the best day so far?

....

....

....

....

....

....

....

....

....

....

....

....

....

....

....

It has been a rough few days but I choose not to focus on the negative, and instead, allow myself to be filled with positive thoughts.

REFLECTION: Write down a list of five positive things in your life today.

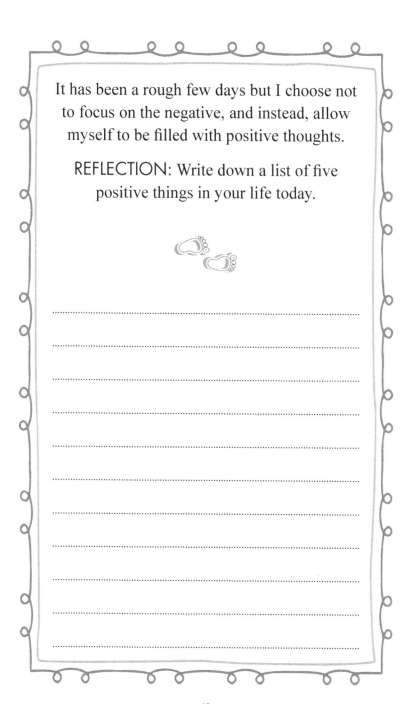

....

....

....

....

....

....

....

....

....

....

Today I left the hospital without my baby, but I look forward to the day when we will go home together.

REFLECTION: What will be the design scheme for your baby's room? Think about it and write it down.

....

....

....

....

....

....

....

....

....

Today my baby lived to see another day, and I am grateful.

REFLECTION: What is the first thing you are going to do with your baby once s/he goes home?

....

....

....

....

....

....

....

....

....

....

I held my baby during skin-to-skin,
and felt the heartbeat on my chest,
and felt at peace with the world.

REFLECTION: Describe what it felt like
to hold your baby for the first time.

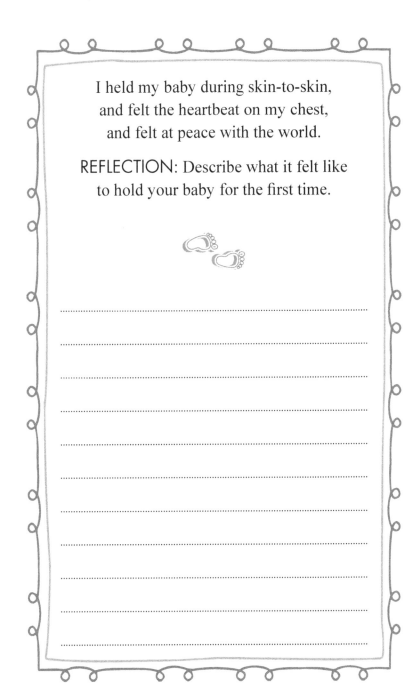

....

....

....

....

....

....

....

....

....

....

I held my baby's hand today,
and s/he knows that I am here,
and that I love her/him.

REFLECTION: Describe one thing that
you can do to show your baby love.

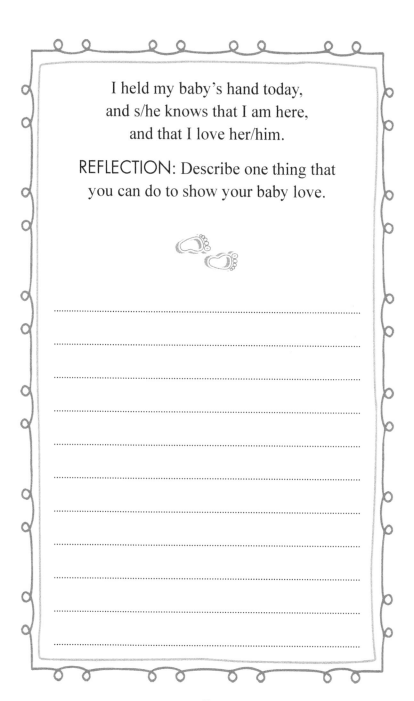

....

....

....

....

....

....

....

....

....

....

Helping with my preemie's care times
is one of the best parts of my day.

REFLECTION: What else do
you look forward to?

....

....

....

....

....

....

....

....

....

....

....

My baby is a fighter, and s/he knows
that I love her/him very much.

REFLECTION: Name one thing
that your baby did today to let
you know s/he is a fighter.

....

....

....

....

....

....

....

....

....

....

Exercise helps me feel good, inside and out.

REFLECTION: Take a break today, and get some exercise. In order to take care of your preemie, you also have to take care of yourself.

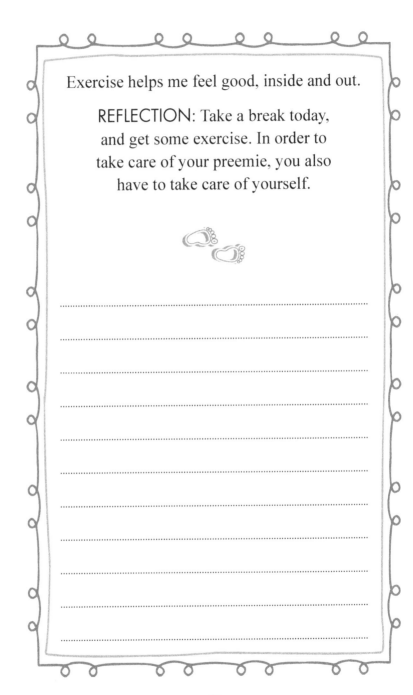

....
....
....
....
....
....
....
....
....
....
....
....

God gave me this baby, and s/he is a blessing.

REFLECTION: Write down one way
your baby has been a blessing.

....

....

....

....

....

....

....

....

....

....

I heard my baby cry for the first time, and it was beautiful!

REFLECTION: Write down another first you have experienced with your baby.

....

....

....

....

....

....

....

....

....

....

....

....

....

I am thankful for the nurses who
take care of my preemie.

REFLECTION: Write down the name
of one nurse you are thankful for.

....

....

....

....

....

....

....

....

....

....

Producing milk is a challenge, but
I will continue to do my best.

REFLECTION: Write down three
things you can do to help with
your milk production.

....

....

....

....

....

....

....

....

....

....

Happiness is a choice,
and it is one that I will keep
choosing every day.

REFLECTION: Write down one
thing that makes you happy.

....

....

....

....

....

....

....

....

....

....

I will receive good news today
about my preemie's progress.

REFLECTION: Write down a recent
piece of good news you received
about your preemie.

....

....

....

....

....

....

....

....

....

....

I am open to receiving all of the blessings
that flow from having this preemie in my life.

REFLECTION: Name one thing that
has changed your life for the better
since your baby has been born.

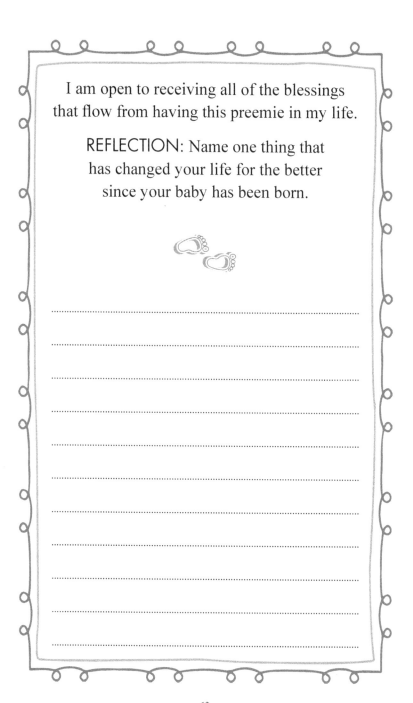

....

....

....

....

....

....

....

....

....

....

My medical team and I are on the same page.

REFLECTION: How did it make you feel to know they understood your concerns?

....

....

....

....

....

....

....

....

....

....

....

My presence in my preemie's room creates a positive, happy place where I can create good memories.

REFLECTION: Name one thing you can do today to create a positive memory.

....

....

....

....

....

....

....

....

....

....

I believe that healing is taking
place for my preemie.

REFLECTION: What helps you to continue
believing that your preemie is healing?

....

....

....

....

....

....

....

....

....

....

....

Every little cell in my preemie's
body is growing.

REFLECTION: Take a moment today
to focus on one group of cells, such as
the heart or the lungs, and say a special
prayer for that part of the body.

....

....

....

....

....

....

....

....

....

I am a great provider for my preemie.

REFLECTION: Write down
one way in which you are a provider.

....

....

....

....

....

....

....

....

....

....

....

I have a good relationship with
my preemie's nurse.

REFLECTION: What makes your preemie's
nurse special? Make a point to say something
positive to your preemie's nurse today.

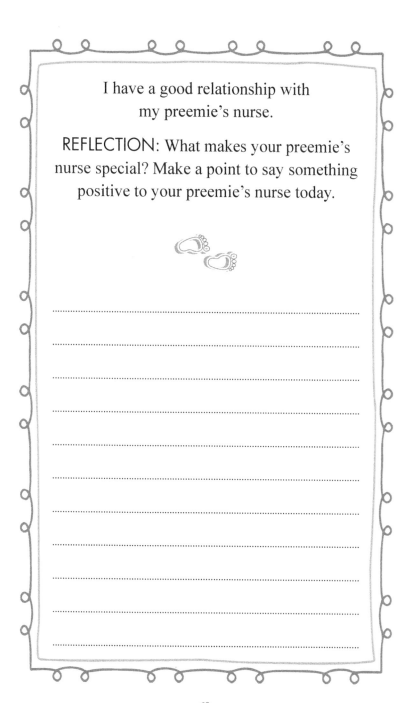

....

....

....

....

....

....

....

....

....

....

I am learning new skills every day.

REFLECTION: What is one skill you have learned that will help you take care of your preemie?

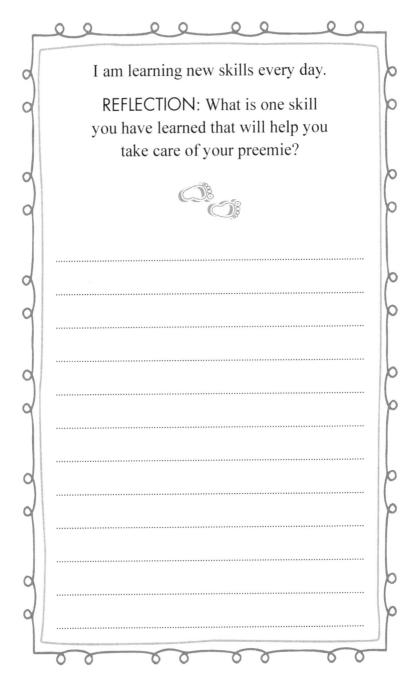

....

....

....

....

....

....

....

....

....

....

....

My little preemie is loved and cared for.

REFLECTION: Name one way you
can show your preemie love.

....

....

....

....

....

....

....

....

....

....

I have confidence in my baby's
medical team!

REFLECTION: Name one positive thing
about your baby's NICU team.

....

....

....

....

....

....

....

....

....

....

....

....

....

Inside my preemie's tiny chest
lies the heart of a champion.

REFLECTION: What is one thing your
baby did today that you are proud of?

....

....

....

....

....

....

....

....

....

....

....

....

The best things come in
small packages.

REFLECTION: Write down your
baby's weight at birth and compare
it to how much s/he weighs now.

....
....
....
....
....
....
....
....
....
....

My preemie is an answer to my prayer, and every day s/he brings me the greatest joy.

REFLECTION: Think about when you first realized you were pregnant, and write down how that made you feel.

....

....

....

....

....

....

....

....

....

....

Today I am rested, relaxed, and rejuvenated.

REFLECTION: What are three things
that you do to recharge after
you leave the hospital?

....

....

....

....

....

....

....

....

....

....

....

....

I appreciate my preemie's doctors.

REFLECTION: Write down
one thing you appreciate about the
doctors caring for your preemie.

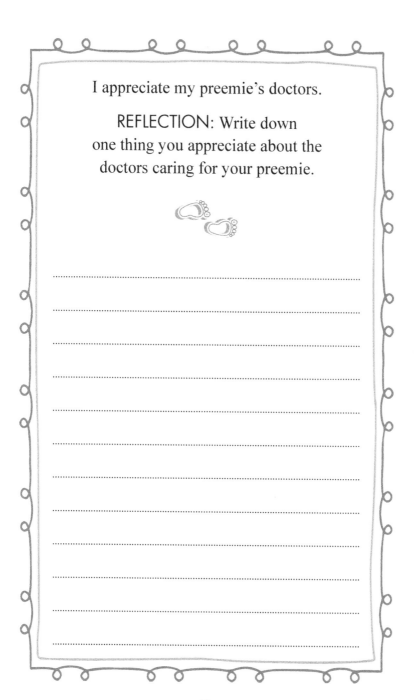

....

....

....

....

....

....

....

....

....

....

I didn't expect to be on this journey,
but I will live it out to the fullest!

REFLECTION: Name one way you
can live life to the fullest.

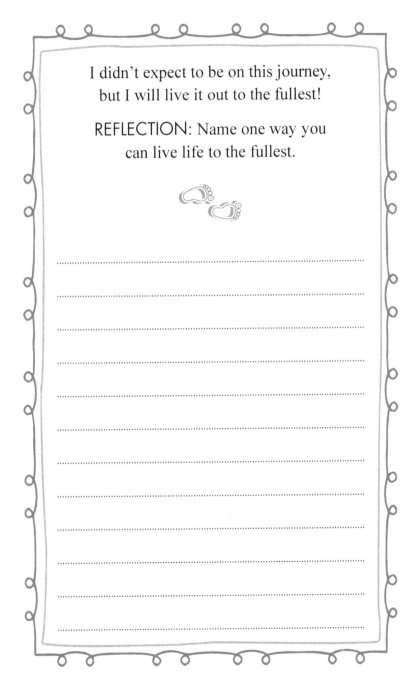

....

....

....

....

....

....

....

....

....

....

....

....

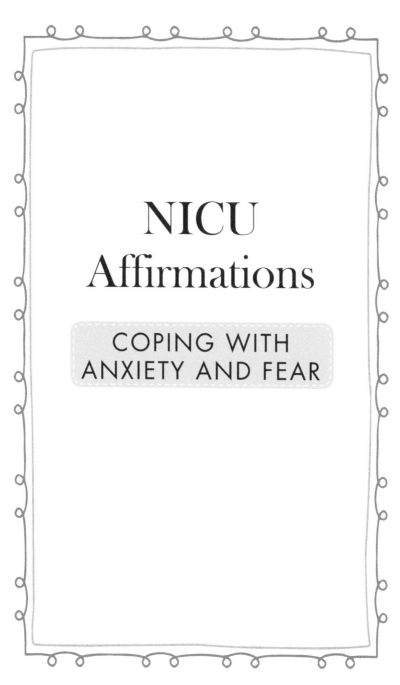

NICU
Affirmations

COPING WITH ANXIETY AND FEAR

My baby is very sick and I don't know everything that's going on, but I am patient and understanding.

REFLECTION: Write down one way you can better understand what's happening with your baby.

....

....

....

....

....

....

....

....

....

....

All the lines and tubes connected to
my baby are scary, but I know they
are helping to keep my baby alive.

REFLECTION: Write down one thing you
don't understand about the lines and tubes,
and ask your baby's doctor about it.

....

....

....

....

....

....

....

....

....

....

I'm afraid, but I believe that
my baby will be okay.

REFLECTION: Name one promise that
will help you believe in your preemie's
development, and write it down.

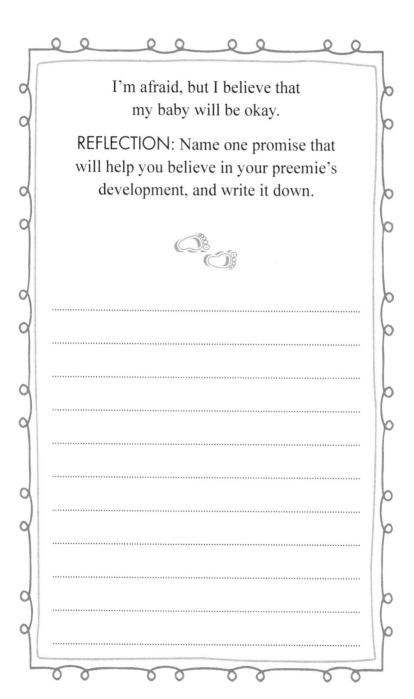

....

....

....

....

....

....

....

....

....

....

I maintain a positive attitude and a good spirit, despite the endless questions by friends and family about my preemie's progress, which remind me how scared I am.

REFLECTION: Write down some pre-planned responses to the most common questions from friends and family.

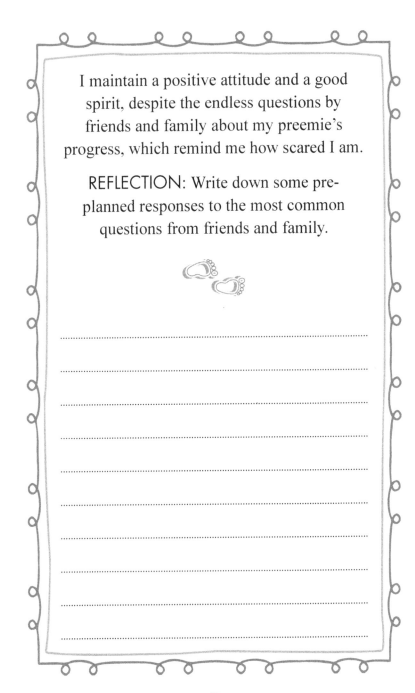

....

....

....

....

....

....

....

....

....

Difficulty breastfeeding does not
make me a failure as a mother.

REFLECTION: Name three ways in
which you are there for your baby.

....

....

....

....

....

....

....

....

....

....

....

....

I am feeling helpless,
but I spent time at my baby's bedside
today and that is enough.

REFLECTION: What did you learn
at your baby's bedside today?

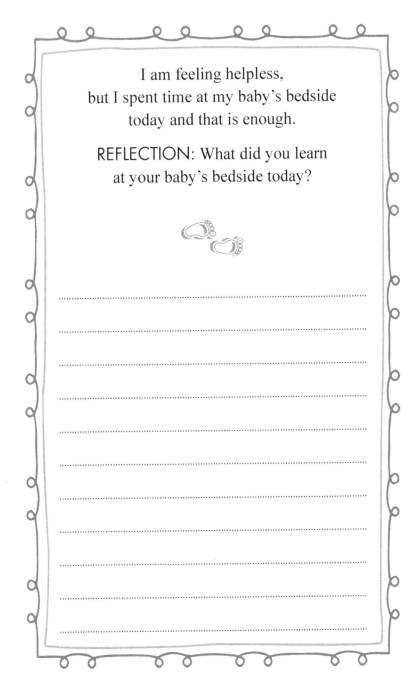

....

....

....

....

....

....

....

....

....

....

I am forming new habits every day that
push me through this experience.

REFLECTION: Write down
one positive new habit that you have
started since your NICU journey.

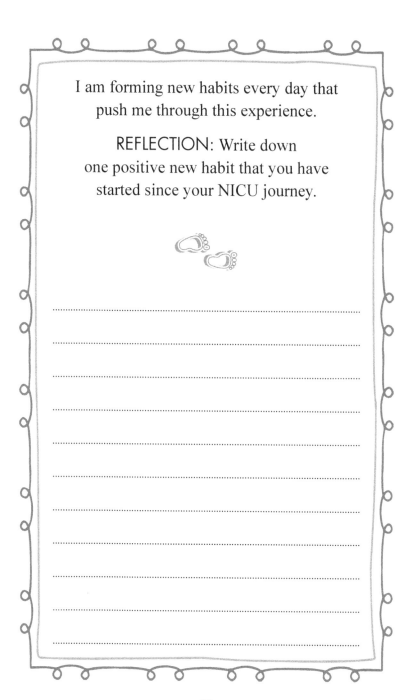

....

....

....

....

....

....

....

....

....

....

....

I don't have to feel powerless;
I can find appropriate ways to
advocate for my preemie.

REFLECTION: Name one way that
you have advocated for your preemie.

....

....

....

....

....

....

....

....

....

....

I will not fear the unexpected, and will allow my preemie the time and space s/he needs to grow and develop.

REFLECTION: How do you remain hopeful during this time?

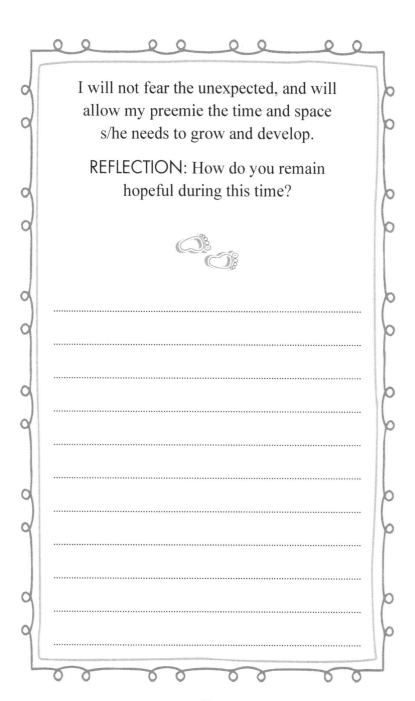

....

....

....

....

....

....

....

....

....

....

I do not have to be bound by guilt
and sadness. I give myself permission
to be optimistic and hopeful.

REFLECTION: What is one thing you
can be optimistic about today?

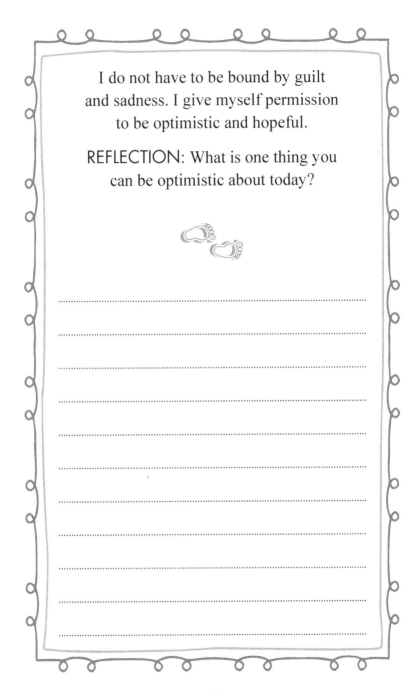

....

....

....

....

....

....

....

....

....

....

Today was emotional and scary, but
my baby and I made it through.

REFLECTION: Say a prayer for
your baby today, and write it down.

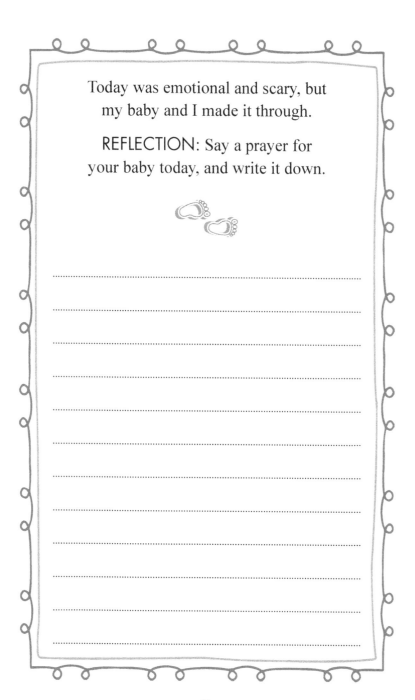

....

....

....

....

....

....

....

....

....

....

....

It is okay to not be okay.

REFLECTION: Who is one person in your life to whom you can admit that you are not okay? Give her/him a call today.

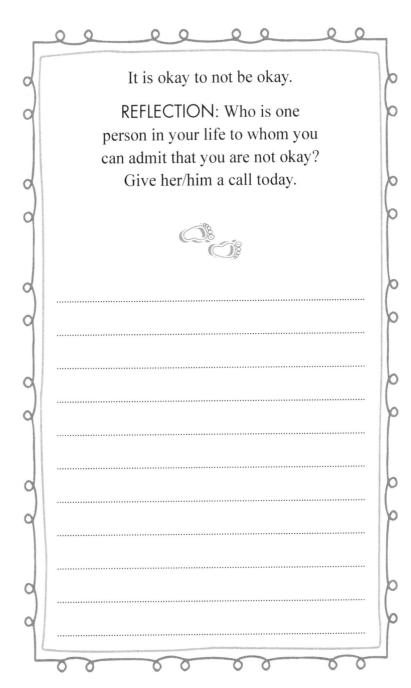

....

....

....

....

....

....

....

....

....

....

Today I refuse to feel stuck and
will push through any obstacle.

REFLECTION: Write down
one obstacle you have overcome
since your preemie was born.

....

....

....

....

....

....

....

....

....

....

....

I will live in this moment, and enjoy it without overwhelming myself with what is to come.

REFLECTION: Write down one thing you can do today to live in the moment.

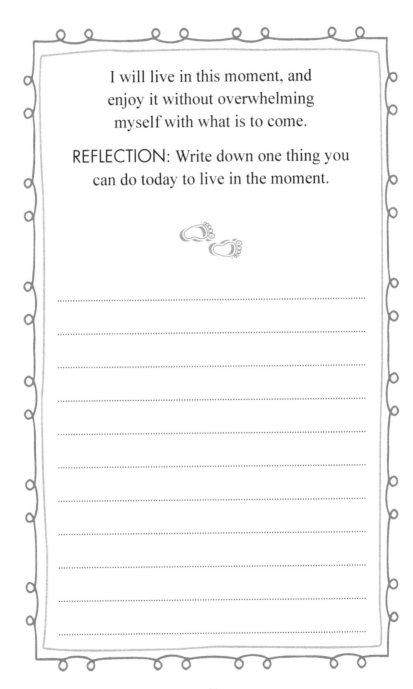

....

....

....

....

....

....

....

....

....

....

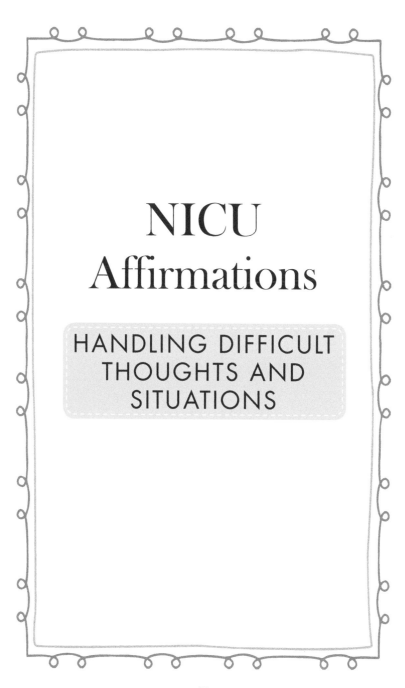

NICU
Affirmations

HANDLING DIFFICULT THOUGHTS AND SITUATIONS

My baby is in the NICU and
it is not my fault.

REFLECTION: Describe one thing you
can do to overcome feelings of guilt.

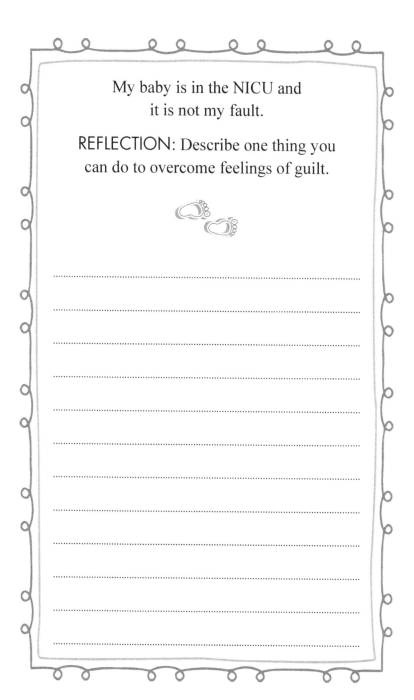

....

....

....

....

....

....

....

....

....

....

....

I have to rest and take care of myself
so that I can be there for my baby.

REFLECTION: Write down one thing you
can do to take care of yourself today.

....

....

....

....

....

....

....

....

....

....

I accept that people don't always know
the right thing to say, but I appreciate their
concern and attempt to provide support.

REFLECTION: What can you do to deal
with people who are unintentionally being
insensitive? If you are experiencing difficulty
with this reach out to your preemie's social
worker or NICU parent support group.

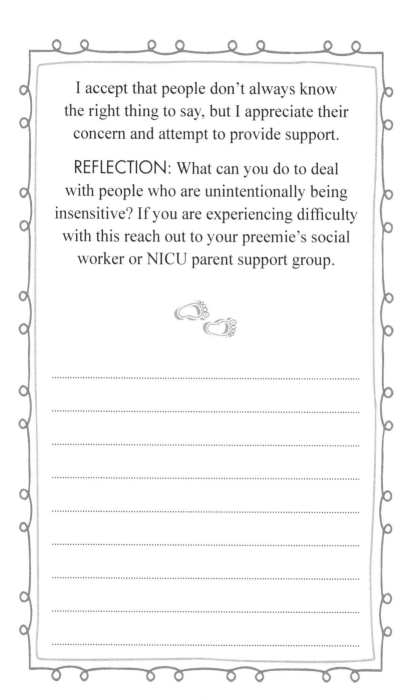

....

....

....

....

....

....

....

....

It is part of my life's calling to go on
this journey with my preemie.

REFLECTION: How does that make you feel?

....

....

....

....

....

....

....

....

....

....

....

....

Home is where my preemie is.

REFLECTION: Where is your preemie right now? How long has s/he been in the NICU?

....

....

....

....

....

....

....

....

....

....

....

I stretch out my arms to God and feel
His love surrounding me. I release
the tension and feel at ease.

REFLECTION: Write down one
burden on your heart that you can
let go and give to God today.

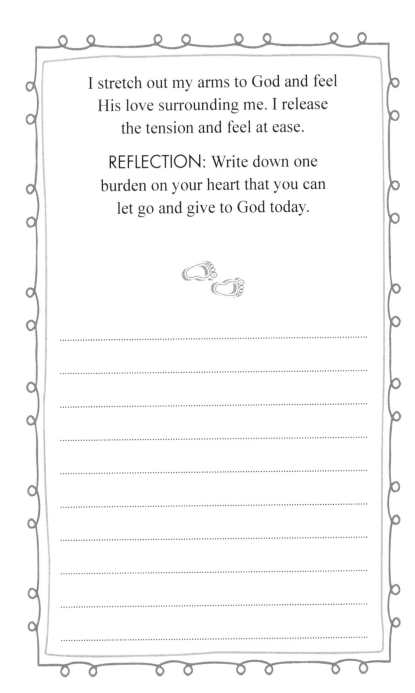

....

....

....

....

....

....

....

....

....

I am a champion for my preemie and
issues that will affect her/ him.

REFLECTION: Write down one way
that you can challenge family and
friends to support preemie issues.

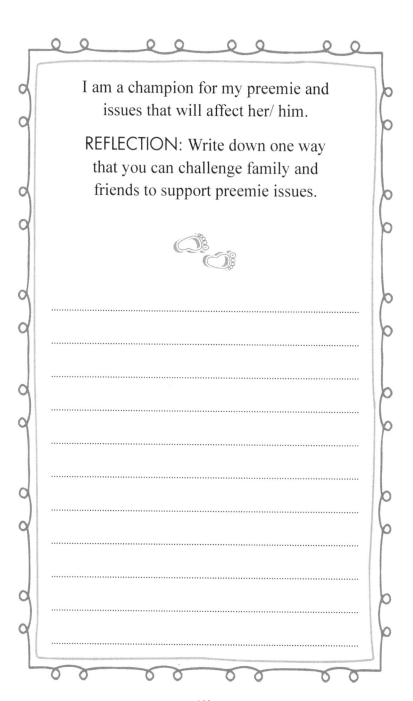

....

....

....

....

....

....

....

....

....

....

I'm leaving the hospital again today without my preemie, but one day we will leave together!

REFLECTION: Write down what helps you get through the times when you have to leave your preemie.

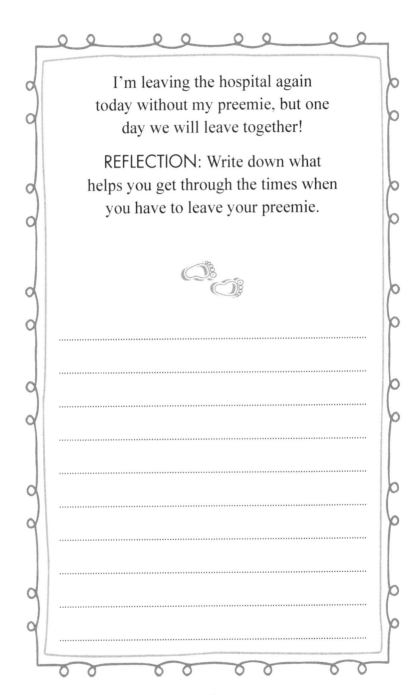

....

....

....

....

....

....

....

....

....

I am a great mom, and I did not cause my baby to deliver early.

REFLECTION: Say this as many times as you need to believe it. Repeat to yourself that you cannot control every outcome. This is not your fault.

....

....

....

....

....

....

....

....

God does not give us more
than we can bear, so I can have faith that
I am strong enough to handle this.

REFLECTION: Name one of your strengths.

....

....

....

....

....

....

....

....

....

....

....

....

I may never understand why, but I can find strength and courage in this journey.

REFLECTION: Name one way you have been courageous since your baby was born.

....
....
....
....
....
....
....
....
....
....
....

I am braver than
I ever thought possible.

REFLECTION: Write down what
you think it means to be brave.

....

....

....

....

....

....

....

....

....

....

....

....

Life for my preemie is exactly
as it is supposed to be.

REFLECTION: How does that
statement make you feel?

....

....

....

....

....

....

....

....

....

....

My baby needs a breathing tube to help her/ him breathe, but today was still a good day.

REFLECTION: Take ten minutes to do a meditation or say a prayer, and be thankful for the machine that helps your baby to breathe.

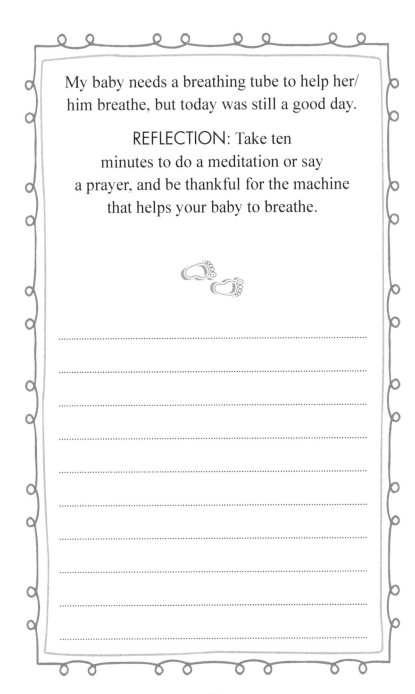

....

....

....

....

....

....

....

....

....

I am going back to work but my baby
is still my number one priority.

REFLECTION: Make a schedule to balance
your time between home and work.

....

....

....

....

....

....

....

....

....

....

I can overcome NICU-ITIS!

REFLECTION: Talking with other moms who have been in your shoes can help! Plan to join a NICU parent support group. If you are already a member, write down one way in which it has helped you cope with this experience.

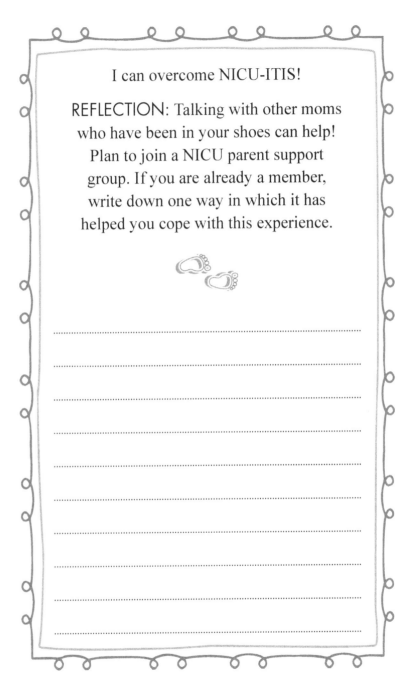

....

....

....

....

....

....

....

....

....

....

Every morning brings a new day, and
this is not the end of our story.

REFLECTION: Name one part of your
journey so far that you want your
baby to know when s/he grows up.

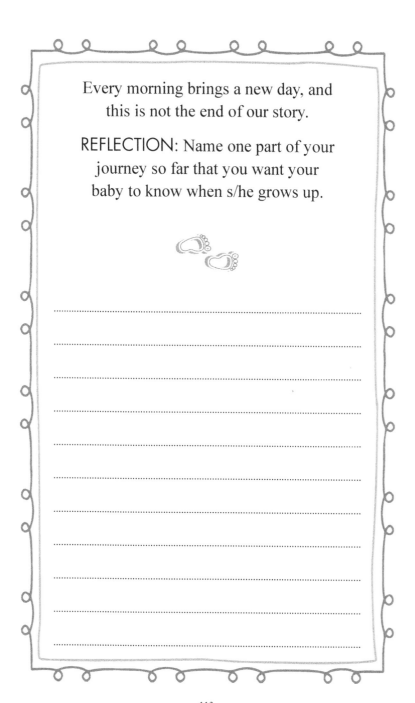

....

....

....

....

....

....

....

....

....

....

I can effectively communicate any concern I have to my NICU team.

REFLECTION: Do you feel a part of the decision making for your preemie? If not, what can you do to be more actively involved?

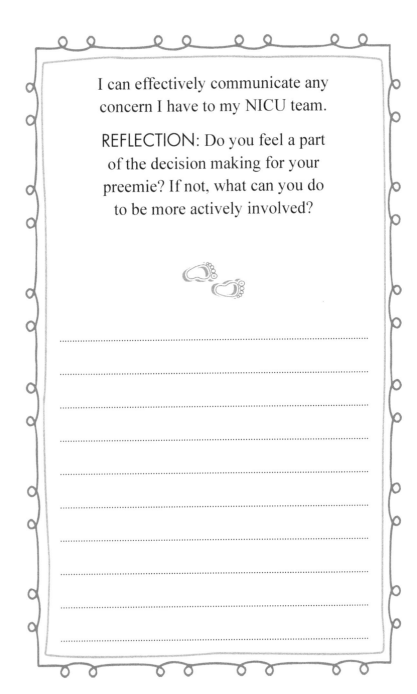

....

....

....

....

....

....

....

....

....

....

It is okay to take a break, and that doesn't make me a bad parent.

REFLECTION: Write down one thing you can do to take a break today.

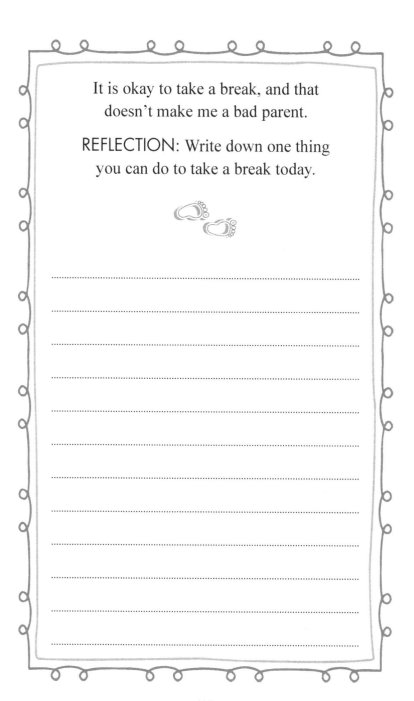

....

....

....

....

....

....

....

....

....

....

....

....

I have the courage to face this day no matter what the outcome may be.

REFLECTION: Name another obstacle that your baby has overcome since birth.

....

....

....

....

....

....

....

....

....

....

....

....

....

....

Not being at home right now with my baby does not make me less of a mom.

REFLECTION: Write down three things that make you an awesome mom!

....

....

....

....

....

....

....

....

....

....

....

....

It is okay to ask for help. Needing help doesn't mean that I don't have it together.

REFLECTION: Write down something that you need help with today, and take action. Ask for help!

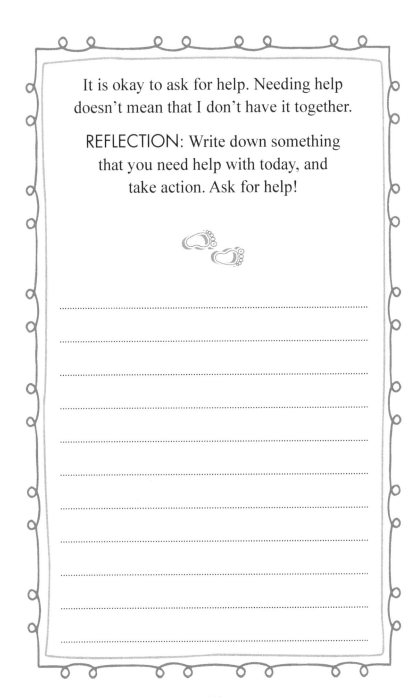

....

....

....

....

....

....

....

....

....

....

I did not expect to deliver early and I now have a preemie, but I remain positive.

REFLECTION: Name one thing you can do to help you through this challenge.

....

....

....

....

....

....

....

....

....

....

....

My baby is not stable today and needs a lot of support, but I can find peace and hope in every moment if I consciously look for it.

REFLECTION: Think back to a moment in your life when you were filled with peace. Write it down.

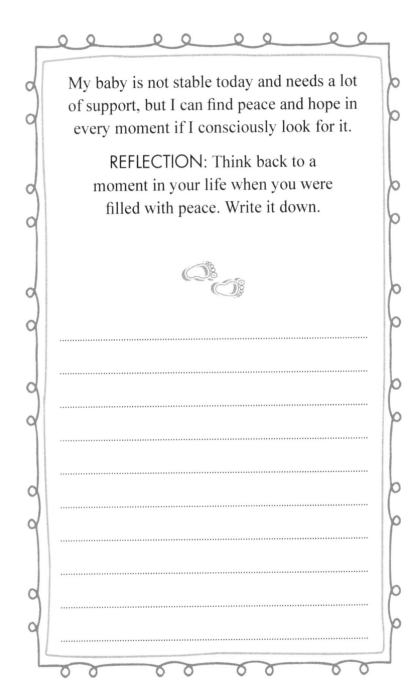

....

....

....

....

....

....

....

....

....

....

I make my baby my number one priority,
even if it means admitting that I need help.

REFLECTION: Write down one thing you do
that shows your baby always comes first.

....

....

....

....

....

....

....

....

....

....

....

Today I release my need to be perfect
and focus on doing my best.

REFLECTION: What is one great thing
you did for your baby today?

....

....

....

....

....

....

....

....

....

....

....

I heard bad news today, but this is not the end, and tomorrow is a new day.

REFLECTION: What is one thing you can look forward to tomorrow?

....

....

....

....

....

....

....

....

....

....

....

I am an informed mother who asks questions about my preemie's care until I feel I understand the treatment being provided. I will do my research to learn more about my preemie's issues.

REFLECTION: List some good resources for you to learn more information about preemies. If you don't have any, ask your preemie's doctor.

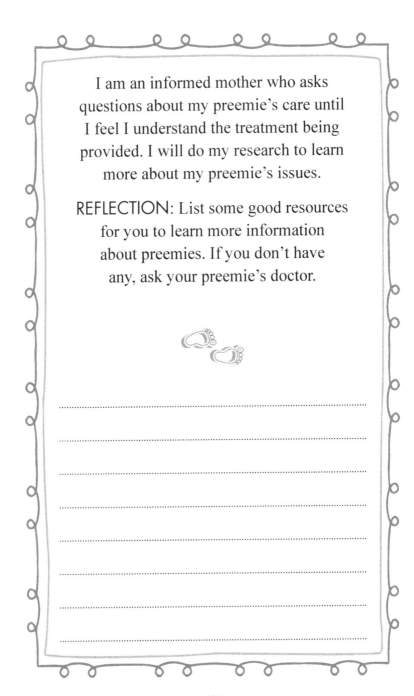

....

....

....

....

....

....

....

I do not have to carry the weight of
this situation all on my shoulders.
I have support and I am loved.

REFLECTION: Write down the
name of someone in your life with
whom you can share your feelings
and call her/him right now.

....

....

....

....

....

....

....

....

....

....

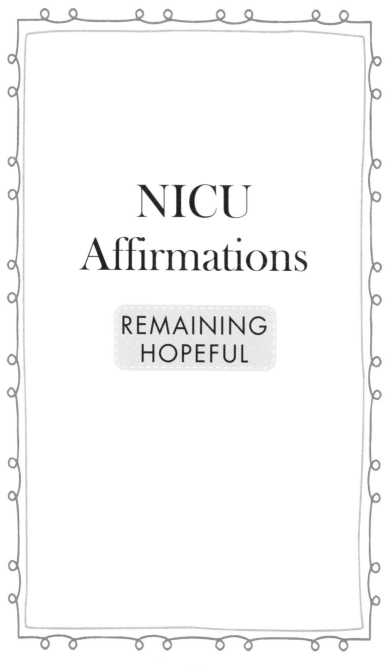

NICU
Affirmations

REMAINING
HOPEFUL

There are no small steps in
the journey to home.

REFLECTION: What is one thing
your baby did today that brings her/
him closer to going home?

....

....

....

....

....

....

....

....

....

....

My baby is sick today, but the treatments
will work and s/he will get well.

REFLECTION: Write down how
your baby's treatment is designed
to help him/her get well.

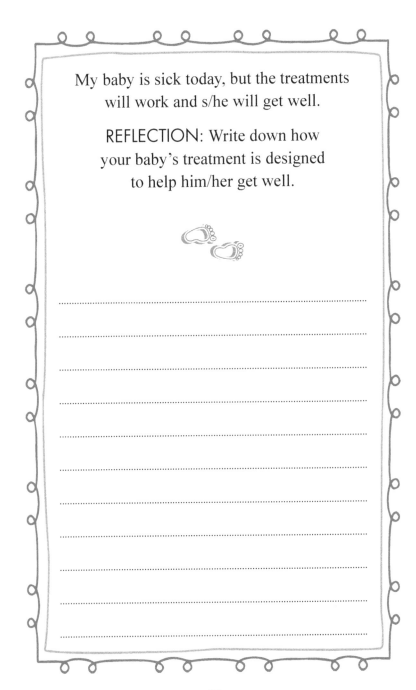

....

....

....

....

....

....

....

....

....

....

....

My baby has all the strength s/
he needs to get better.

REFLECTION: What do you do to
help your family remain optimistic
about your baby's development?

....

....

....

....

....

....

....

....

....

....

I am strong, and every day we are one
step closer to being discharged.

REFLECTION: Give one example of how
you have displayed strength on this journey.

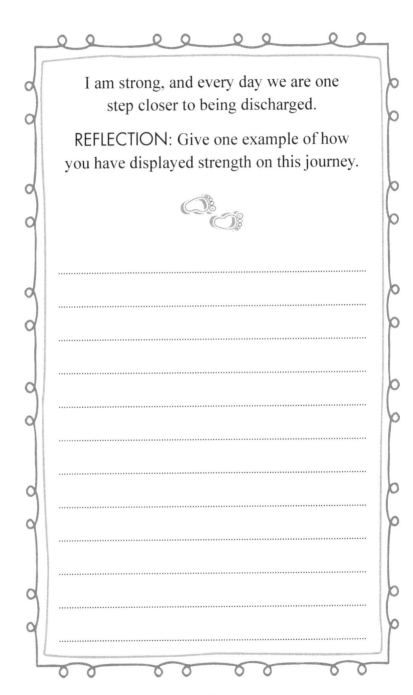

....

....

....

....

....

....

....

....

....

....

....

....

Today was a challenge, but we made
it through to fight another day.

REFLECTION: Reflect on one challenge your
baby had since birth that s/he has overcome.

....

....

....

....

....

....

....

....

....

....

....

I trust in my ability to advocate for my baby.

REFLECTION: Write down one way you have contributed to your baby's care.

....

....

....

....

....

....

....

....

....

....

....

....

I am just the right mother for this preemie.

REFLECTION: What makes you
the best mom for this baby?

....

....

....

....

....

....

....

....

....

....

....

My preemie's diagnosis is not
what I expected, but we will get
through this as a family.

REFLECTION: What resources can
you use for help? Write them down.

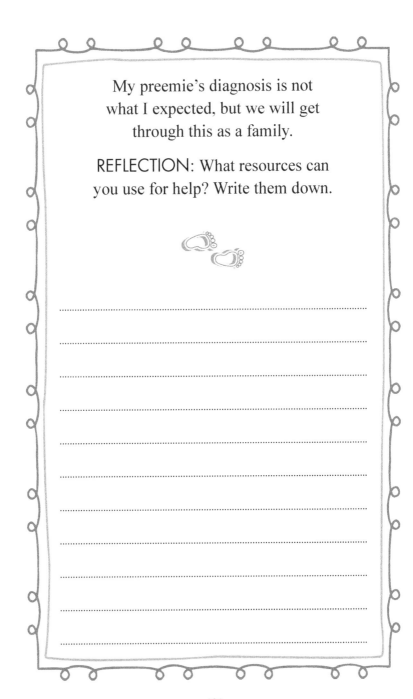

....

....

....

....

....

....

....

....

....

....

Today is a new day, and I am not bound by yesterday's mistakes.

REFLECTION: Name one thing you will not be bound by today.

....

....

....

....

....

....

....

....

....

....

....

This baby is my heart and soul, and every day I claim great things for her/him.

REFLECTION: Name the thing you want most for your preemie today.

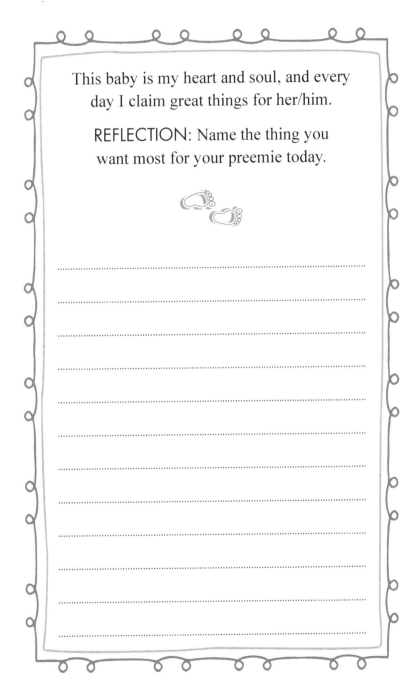

....

....

....

....

....

....

....

....

....

....

....

My preemie is in God's hands
and He is in control.

REFLECTION: Write down one way that
God has shown you that He is in control.

....

....

....

....

....

....

....

....

....

....

....

May God bless my preemie's lungs and grow them and make them strong.

REFLECTION: Name one way your baby has shown improvement in her/his lungs.

....

....

....

....

....

....

....

....

....

....

....

....

My preemie has changed me and
I will never be the same.

REFLECTION: Name one way this
experience has changed you for the better.

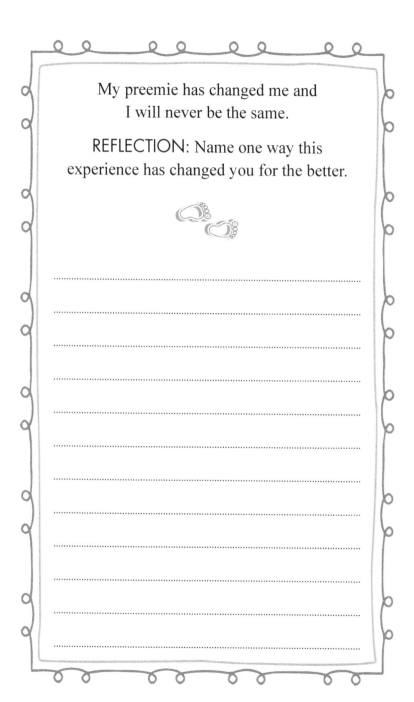

....

....

....

....

....

....

....

....

....

....

....

....

When circumstances seem immovable, I call on God Who is the ultimate Way-Maker.

REFLECTION: When else has God made a way for you or your family?

....

....

....

....

....

....

....

....

....

....

....

I have hope for the future and I
am filled with expectation.

REFLECTION: Name one thing that you
are looking forward to in the future.

....

....

....

....

....

....

....

....

....

....

A miracle will happen for my preemie.

REFLECTION: Write down what
a miracle means to you.

....

....

....

....

....

....

....

....

....

....

....

....

I have great family and friends
who support me.

REFLECTION: Write down a list of all the
people you are thankful to have in your life.

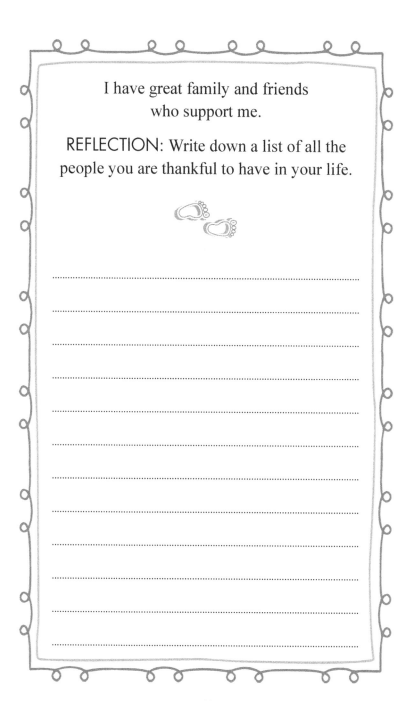

....

....

....

....

....

....

....

....

....

....

....

....

Today's setback will be tomorrow's victory.

REFLECTION: Write down one area of your life where you overcame a challenge through persistence, and describe it.

....

....

....

....

....

....

....

....

....

....

....

....

The end of this hospital stay is in sight,
and I am filled with excitement.

REFLECTION: How are you preparing
for your preemie to come home?

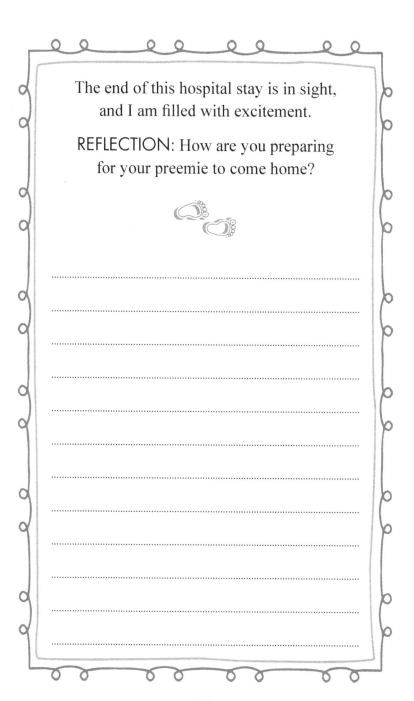

....

....

....

....

....

....

....

....

....

....

....

Watching my preemie fight
fills me with inspiration.

REFLECTION: Who or what else
inspires you? Write it down.

....

....

....

....

....

....

....

....

....

....

....

....

....

....

I am crying today, but my tomorrow
can be filled with laughter.

REFLECTION: Name one thing that always
makes you laugh, and write it down.

....

....

....

....

....

....

....

....

....

....

....

....

My preemie may be in the hospital
but I can still make today special!

REFLECTION: What can you do to
celebrate the holidays with your preemie?

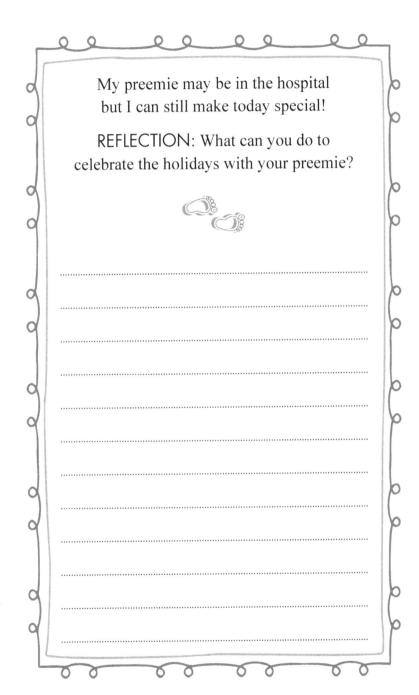

....

....

....

....

....

....

....

....

....

....

....

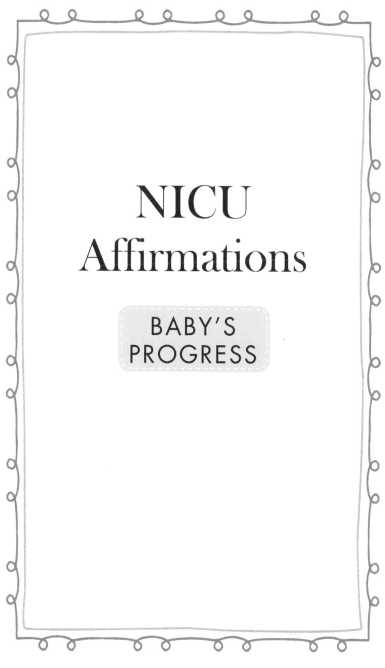

NICU
Affirmations

BABY'S
PROGRESS

My baby knows my smell and is
comforted by my presence.

REFLECTION: Write down one thing
that helps you to feel comforted.

....

....

....

....

....

....

....

....

....

....

....

....

I know my preemie hears and
recognizes my voice.

REFLECTION: Think of your favorite
lullaby that you would like to sing to
your baby, and write down the words.
Start singing it to your baby.

....

....

....

....

....

....

....

....

....

Watching my preemie transform
before my eyes is amazing!

REFLECTION: What is
your preemie's most recent
achievement?

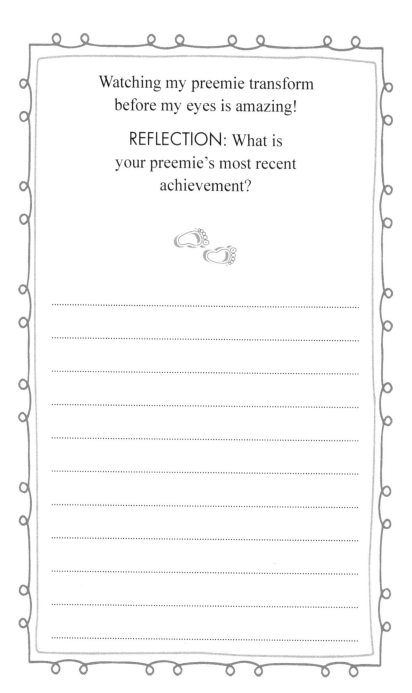

....

....

....

....

....

....

....

....

....

....

My baby breastfed for the first time today,
and I know we have a special bond.

REFLECTION: Think about how you feel
when you get to bond with your baby,
and write this feeling/memory down.

....

....

....

....

....

....

....

....

....

....

Today my baby started feeds,
and I am happy about the progress.

REFLECTION: What is one
more thing you can look forward
to in your baby's journey?

....

....

....

....

....

....

....

....

....

....

My preemie gets better at eating every day.

REFLECTION: How often is your
preemie eating by mouth? How
much of the feed is s/he taking?

....
....
....
....
....
....
....
....
....
....
....
....

My baby took her/his first full bottle today, and I am a proud mom.

REFLECTION: Write down one thing that makes you proud to be a mom.

....

....

....

....

....

....

....

....

....

....

....

My preemie gets closer and
closer to term every day.

REFLECTION: What signs have you noticed
that show your preemie is growing?

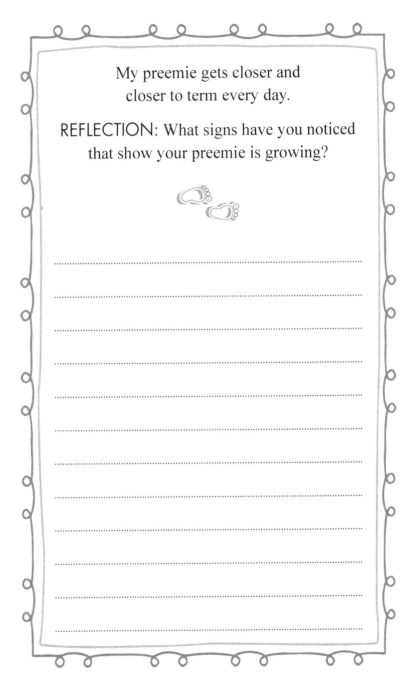

....

....

....

....

....

....

....

....

....

....

....

....

My preemie has overcome another hurdle
with more to go, but I have faith.

REFLECTION: What grows your faith?

....

....

....

....

....

....

....

....

....

....

....

Even baby steps still move
your preemie forward.

REFLECTION: What small step
forward did your baby make today?

....

....

....

....

....

....

....

....

....

....

....

....

My baby is resilient!

REFLECTION: Name one way in
which your baby has been resilient.

....

....

....

....

....

....

....

....

....

....

....

My baby is making great strides, and
I know s/he will be home soon.

REFLECTION: Write down one way your
baby is one step closer to going home.

....

....

....

....

....

....

....

....

....

....

....

....

I see a light at the end of the tunnel,
and it is shining brightly!

REFLECTION: Write down how close
your preemie is to going home.

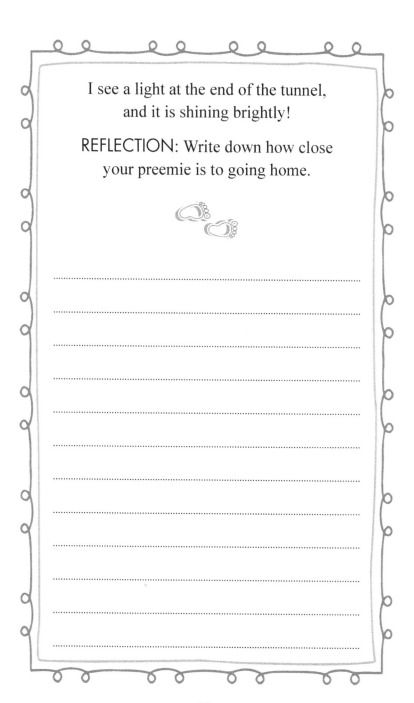

....

....

....

....

....

....

....

....

....

....

....

....

I am filled with gratitude for all that has been done for my preemie in the NICU.

REFLECTION: Write down what you will remember most about your experience in the NICU.

....

....

....

....

....

....

....

....

....

....

....

It is time to take my baby home, and I am filled with excitement and joy!

REFLECTION: Write down how it feels to finally leave the hospital with your baby to go home. List one way you will celebrate this accomplishment.

....

....

....

....

....

....

....

....

....

....

Home Affirmations

ACCOMPLISHMENTS

We made it through the first night home, and I am filled with pride.

REFLECTION: Write down one new goal for you and your baby to accomplish by the end of the week

....

....

....

....

....

....

....

....

....

....

I am a survivor because I have gone on this journey, and I can now be an example for other moms just like me.

REFLECTION: What can you do to support other preemie moms like you who still have babies in the hospital?

....

....

....

....

....

....

....

....

....

....

I couldn't have made it through this journey without my number one partner!

REFLECTION: Name one way your partner has been there for you during this experience.

....

....

....

....

....

....

....

....

....

....

....

....

My baby had her/his first cold,
but I knew what to do.

REFLECTION: Reflect on what made you
most scared to bring your baby home.
Write down how you overcame that.

....

....

....

....

....

....

....

....

....

....

Despite the oxygen, machines, and/or tubes, getting home is still a victory!

REFLECTION: What do you love most about being at home with your preemie?

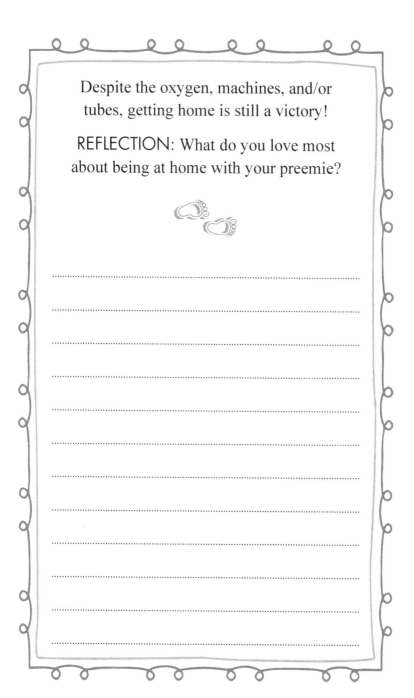

....

....

....

....

....

....

....

....

....

....

....

I have created a nurturing environment to help my preemie grow, develop, and feel cherished.

REFLECTION: Write down what nurturing means to you.

....

....

....

....

....

....

....

....

....

....

I embrace gratitude and let go of blame and negative self-talk.

REFLECTION: Find someone you are thankful for and express your gratitude to her/him today.

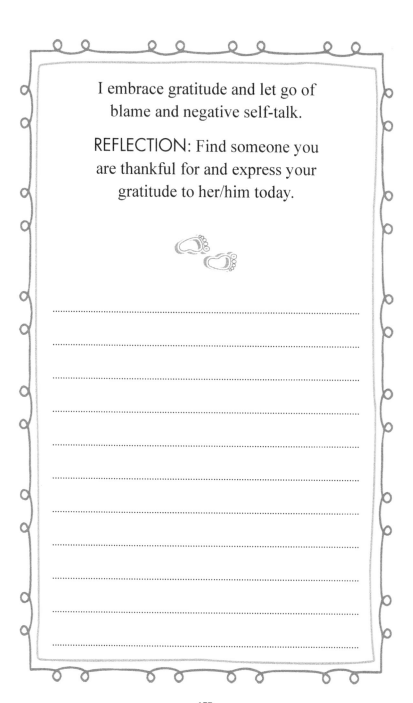

....

....

....

....

....

....

....

....

....

....

I have the freedom to be my
authentic self at all times.

REFLECTION: Who in your life
accepts you for who you are?

....
....
....
....
....
....
....
....
....
....
....
....

The first family trip was an
ordeal but it was worth it!

REFLECTION: Write down your favorite
part of your first family outing.

....

....

....

....

....

....

....

....

....

....

....

I gain knowledge from my mistakes.

REFLECTION: What lessons have you learned from any past mistakes?

....

....

....

....

....

....

....

....

....

....

....

....

I have what it takes to accept
life's challenges.

REFLECTION: What routines do you
practice to help you persevere?

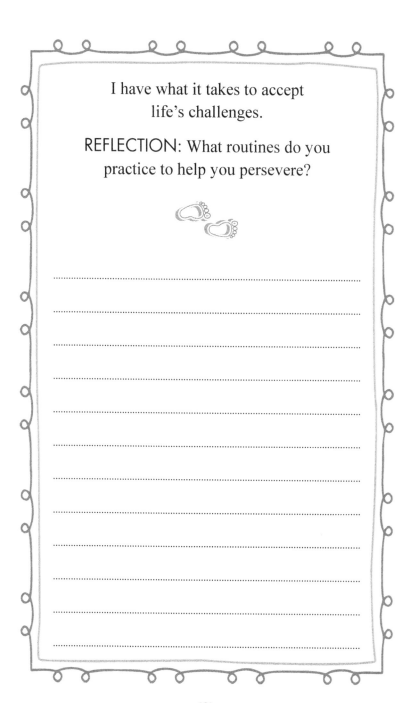

....

....

....

....

....

....

....

....

....

....

....

I have the freedom to
put my family first.

REFLECTION: What is one thing
you have done to let your family
know you put them first?

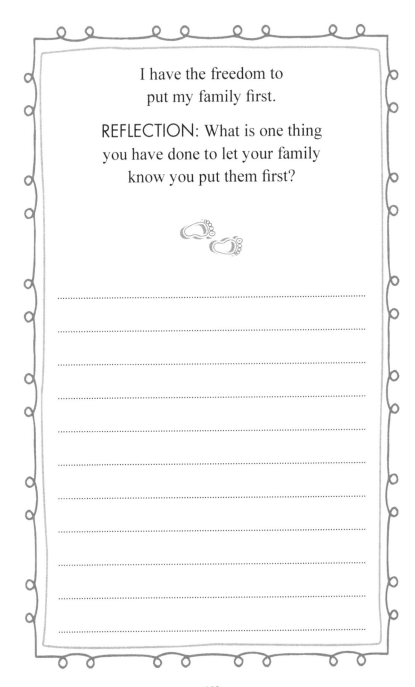

....

....

....

....

....

....

....

....

....

....

....

....

My preemie is growing stronger
and stronger every day!

REFLECTION: As your preemie grows
strong, you do too! Write down five words
that are confidence builders for you.

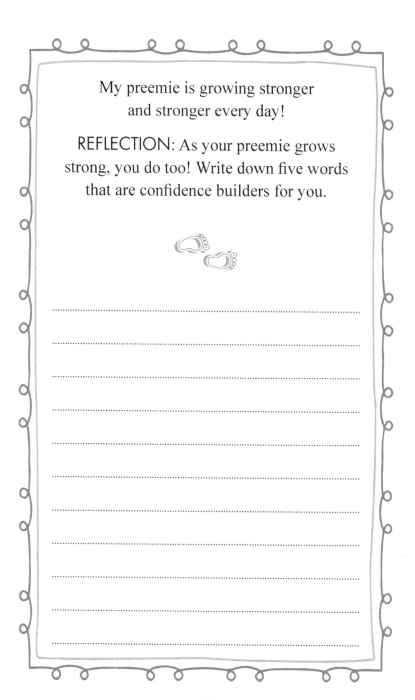

....

....

....

....

....

....

....

....

....

....

My baby is safe and secure.

REFLECTION: What makes you
feel safe? Write it down.

....

....

....

....

....

....

....

....

....

....

....

....

....

....

....

I have balance in my home and in my life.

REFLECTION: What helps
you to create balance?

....

....

....

....

....

....

....

....

....

....

....

I can be as flexible as needed to
work towards my goals.

REFLECTION: How has flexibility
changed your perspective in life?

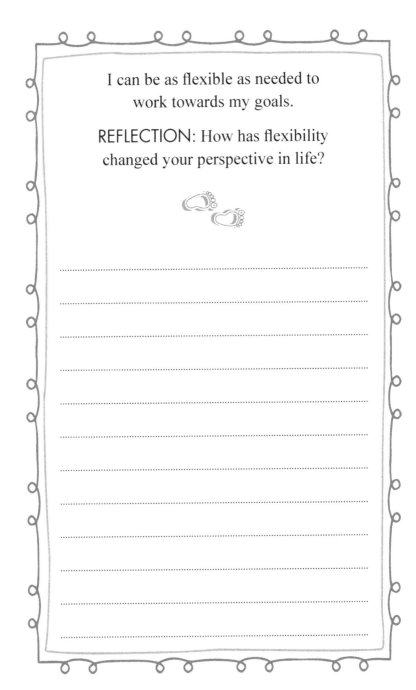

....

....

....

....

....

....

....

....

....

....

....

....

I am doing my very best for
my baby each day.

REFLECTION: What keeps you motivated?

....

....

....

....

....

....

....

....

....

....

I am fearless!

REFLECTION: How do you work to overcome fear in your life?

....

....

....

....

....

....

....

....

....

....

....

....

....

....

....

....

I ignore distractions,
and I keep pressing on.

REFLECTION: Name some
distractions in your life.
How can you remove them?

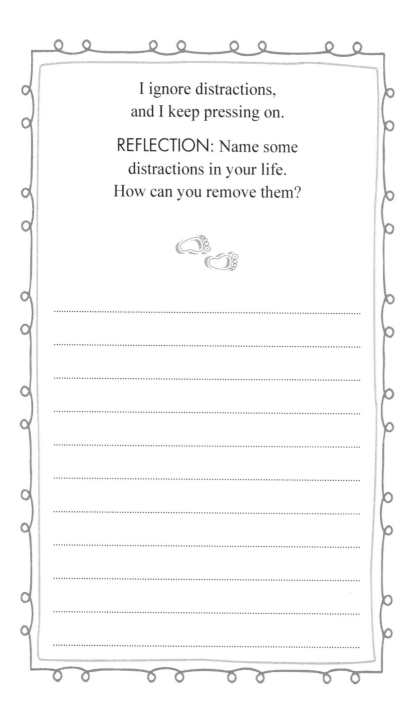

....

....

....

....

....

....

....

....

....

....

I am in a constant state of calm, and ready to face whatever comes my way.

REFLECTION: Write down one thing that helps you to remain focused and calm.

....

....

....

....

....

....

....

....

....

....

There is no right or wrong way to be
a mother to my preemie.
I am doing an excellent job!

REFLECTION: This experience is a
process with a steep learning curve. Name
one thing you have learned today.

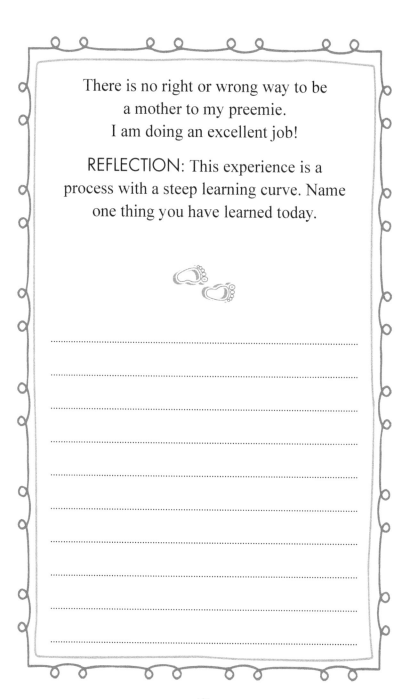

....

....

....

....

....

....

....

....

....

My baby has come a long way and is growing so much every day!

REFLECTION: What milestones has your baby reached since discharge from the NICU? Write them down.

....

....

....

....

....

....

....

....

....

....

It is a privilege to parent and
raise this amazing baby.

REFLECTION: What steps
do you take to help bring
about her/his success?

....

....

....

....

....

....

....

....

....

....

Every day I am becoming the
person I want to be.

REFLECTION: What do you do
to help with self-growth?

....

....

....

....

....

....

....

....

....

....

....

I am in tune with my baby's needs,
and try to meet them as best I can.

REFLECTION: What is one thing your
baby communicated to you today?

....

....

....

....

....

....

....

....

....

....

....

I have an abundance of patience.

REFLECTION: What helps
you to keep your cool?

....

....

....

....

....

....

....

....

....

....

....

I have the courage to fight for my dreams.

REFLECTION: Think about one obstacle that is in the way of obtaining your dream. Visualize yourself overcoming it.

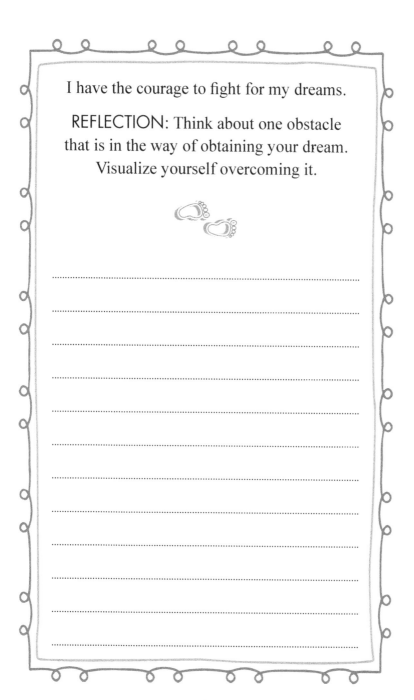

....

....

....

....

....

....

....

....

....

....

....

....

My baby is unique, and I discover more about her/him every day.

REFLECTION: What is special about your baby's disposition?

....

....

....

....

....

....

....

....

....

....

....

....

I am confident in my skills as a mom.

REFLECTION: What skills have you learned since delivering your preemie?

....

....

....

....

....

....

....

....

....

....

Home
Affirmations

GRATITUDE

We are both home, and I am grateful and I accept that a new journey is beginning.

REFLECTION: How are you prepared to handle the journey ahead?

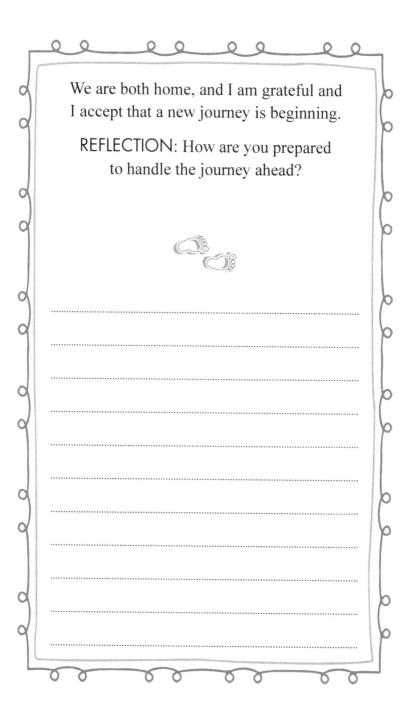

....

....

....

....

....

....

....

....

....

....

I am blessed and thankful for all the support from family and friends during the most difficult times of this journey.

REFLECTION: Take some time right now to compile a gratitude list by writing down all the people and things you have been grateful for during your journey. When you are having a hard day, take this list out and reread it so you can remember all that you have to be thankful for.

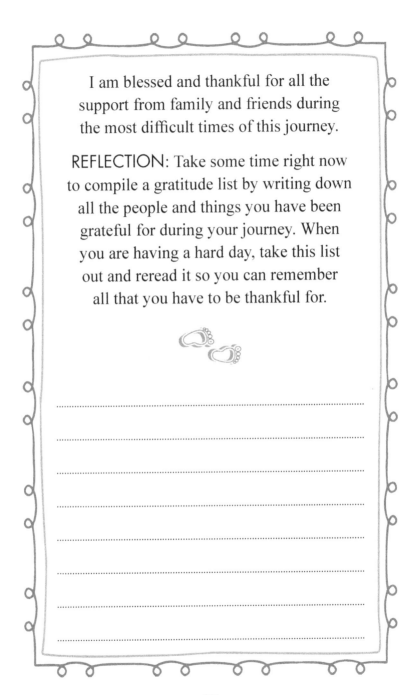

....

....

....

....

....

....

....

....

I appreciate every person in my life.

REFLECTION: In honor
of those who are supporting you,
which person in your life needs you
to be there for her/him today?

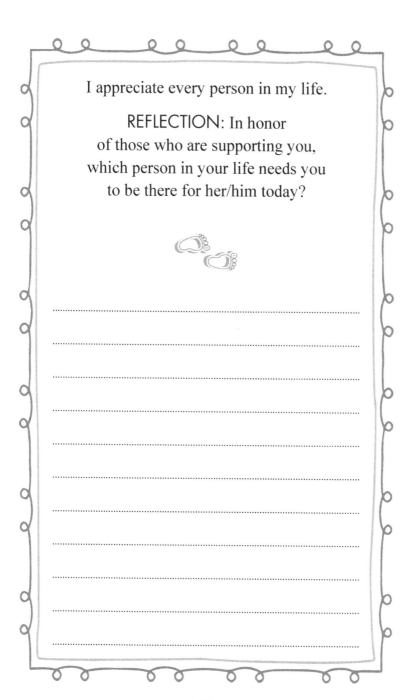

....

....

....

....

....

....

....

....

....

I wake up every day with a
heart full of appreciation.

REFLECTION: What are you
most grateful for right now?

....

....

....

....

....

....

....

....

....

....

....

....

I am thankful to be alive today!

REFLECTION: Write down five
things you are thankful for.

I'm not perfect,
but my baby still loves me.

REFLECTION: How does it make you
feel to have your baby's love?

....

....

....

....

....

....

....

....

....

....

Today I have
so much to be thankful for.

REFLECTION: Write down three things
you are thankful for on today.

....

....

....

....

....

....

....

....

....

....

My preemie is so special, and I am overjoyed to have her/him in my life.

REFLECTION: Name one special quality about your preemie.

....

....

....

....

....

....

....

....

....

....

....

....

I am thankful for every good
thing that comes to me.

REFLECTION: Name one good thing
that has happened to you this week.

....

....

....

....

....

....

....

....

....

....

....

I stand in awe of my baby and all s/he
has been through. I am truly blessed.

REFLECTION: If you have visited the NICU
since discharge, think about how it made you
feel to have everyone see the progress your
baby has made. Write down this memory.

....

....

....

....

....

....

....

....

....

I am the luckiest person because I get
to be the mother of _____.

REFLECTION: Write down one reason why
your baby is lucky to have you for a mom.

....

....

....

....

....

....

....

....

....

....

Going through a battle can leave you with scars, but it is still a blessing to win.

REFLECTION: What scars do you carry from this experience?

....

....

....

....

....

....

....

....

....

....

....

....

Whatever the future holds, this baby is and will continue to be one of the best things in my life!

REFLECTION: Name one way your baby has improved your life.

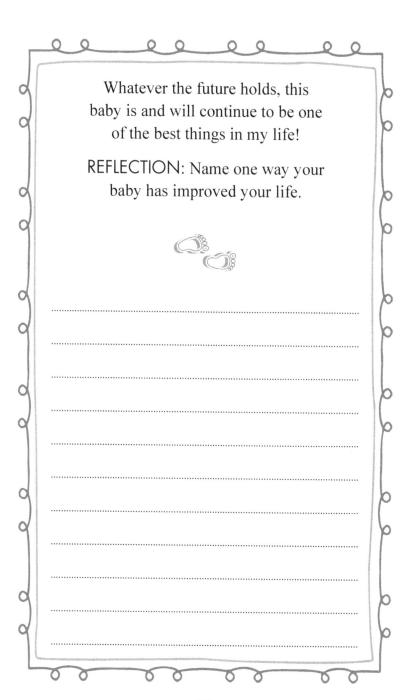

....

....

....

....

....

....

....

....

....

....

Being a mother is an honor that
I do not take for granted.

REFLECTION: Who in your circle
also desires to be a mother? Say a
prayer for that person right now!

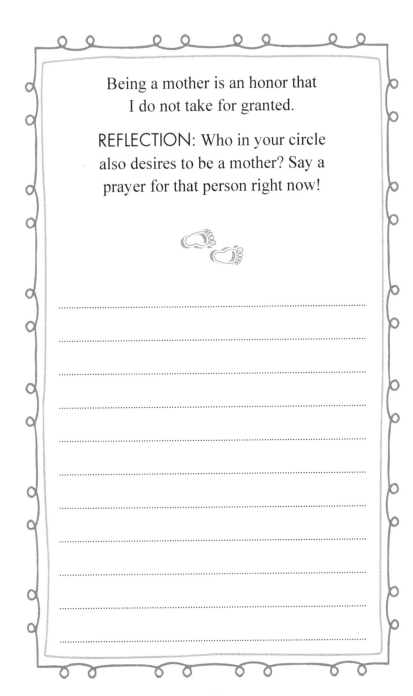

....

....

....

....

....

....

....

....

....

....

Going home with a preemie on oxygen
and monitors feels overwhelming,
but our family can do it!

REFLECTION: How can you and your partner
tag team to take care of your preemie?

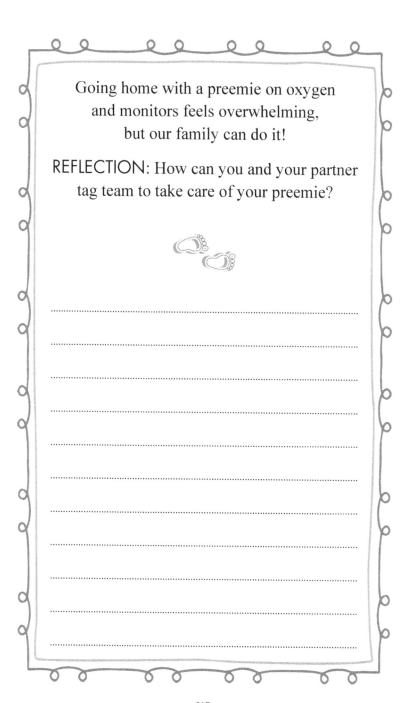

....

....

....

....

....

....

....

....

....

....

Tummy time
with my little one reminds me of all
the blessings we have both shared.

REFLECTION: Write down one way you
can be a blessing to someone else.

....

....

....

....

....

....

....

....

....

....

Each milestone my baby
reaches is a blessing!

REFLECTION: What is your baby's
most recently achieved milestone?

....

....

....

....

....

....

....

....

....

....

My baby is a beautiful gift.

REFLECTION: Write down one beautiful
thing about your baby that you love.

....

....

....

....

....

....

....

....

....

....

....

....

My home is filled with love,
laughter, and light.

REFLECTION: Write down one thing
that makes your home inviting.

....

....

....

....

....

....

....

....

....

....

....

Today all of my family met my baby
for the first time after discharge. I
am filled with positive emotions!

REFLECTION: Write down this memory,
print out a picture that reminds you of these
positive emotions, and paste it here to share
with your little one when s/he is older.

....

....

....

....

....

....

....

....

....

Life is a gift and I will live it to the fullest!

REFLECTION: Name one thing you
can do to live your life more fully.

....

....

....

....

....

....

....

....

....

....

....

Remembering family moments brings me joy.

REFLECTION: Jot down a story about one of your family members that you will one day share with your preemie.

....

....

....

....

....

....

....

....

....

....

....

....

Home
Affirmations

IT'S ALL ABOUT
PERSPECTIVE

I am feeling overwhelmed with
all the appointments is okay, but I
remind myself that they are important
to ensure my baby's health.

REFLECTION: Name one
follow-up appointment you have
had. Write down one good thing that
came out of your appointment.

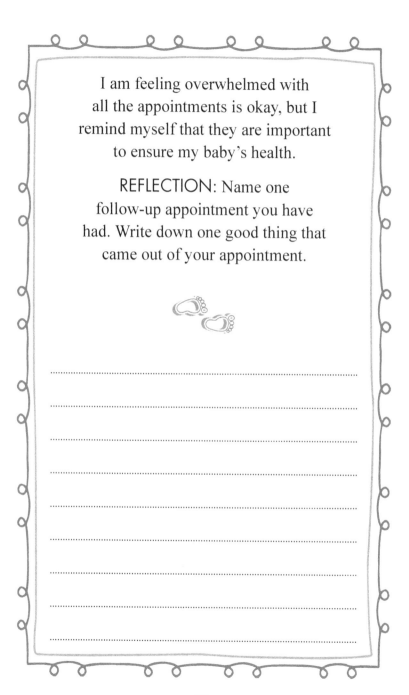

....

....

....

....

....

....

....

....

When I spend time with my little one, the world stops and I focus all my energy and attention on her/him.

REFLECTION: How do you make spending quiet time with your baby a priority?

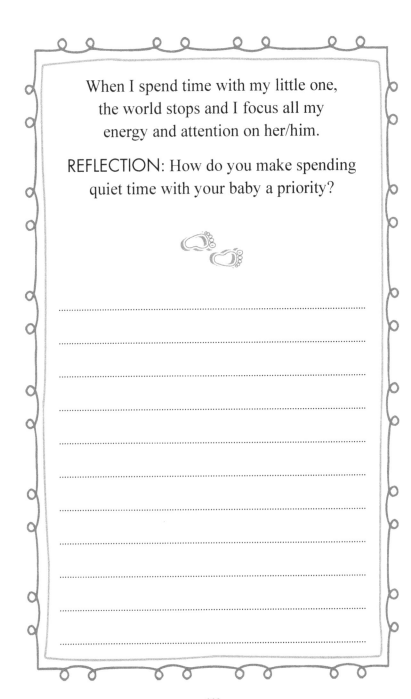

....

....

....

....

....

....

....

....

....

....

I accept that sometimes I will feel guilty,
but then I let it go and move on.

REFLECTION: Write down all of the things
that make you feel guilty on a piece of paper.
Then tear it up, throw it away, and move on.

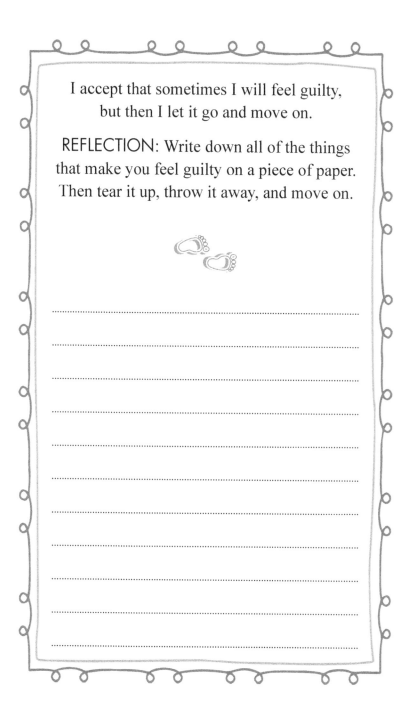

....

....

....

....

....

....

....

....

....

....

I release my worries, and allow
myself to be filled with hope.

REFLECTION: Look up five quotes
about hope and write them down.
Look back at them from time-to-time
when you need encouragement.

....

....

....

....

....

....

....

....

....

....

I deserve grace.

REFLECTION: Who else
can you show grace?

....

....

....

....

....

....

....

....

....

....

I am a teacher, and it is my job
to guide this baby in life.

REFLECTION: Name one
thing that you want to make sure
your baby learns as s/he grows.

....

....

....

....

....

....

....

....

....

....

....

I will not let negative talk enter into
my space and overwhelm my spirit.

REFLECTION: Name one way
you can rephrase negative talk
and avoid negative people.

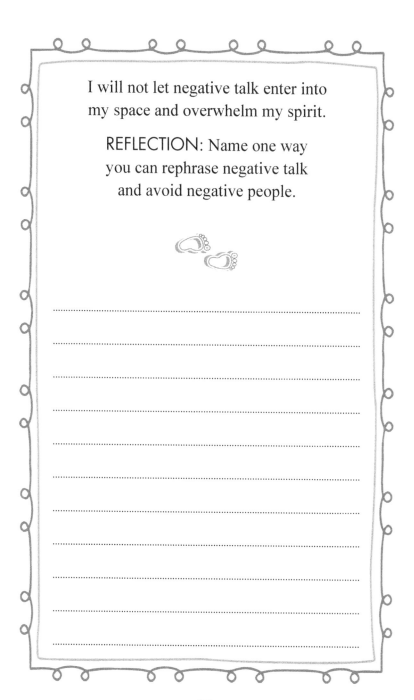

....

....

....

....

....

....

....

....

....

....

My baby is small but that is one
of her/his superpowers.

REFLECTION: How do you handle
questions about how small your
baby is after you are at home?

....

....

....

....

....

....

....

....

....

....

I will not fear change!

REFLECTION: Name one time when change in your life worked out for the better.

....

....

....

....

....

....

....

....

....

....

Some days at home are harder than others, but my baby and I have the strength to overcome.

REFLECTION: Name one thing that makes a hard day easier to endure. Write it down.

....

....

....

....

....

....

....

....

....

....

It is okay to get frustrated at times
when caring for my baby. This does
not make me a bad parent.

REFLECTION: What can you do right
now to help relieve any stress you might
be feeling? Put a plan in place.

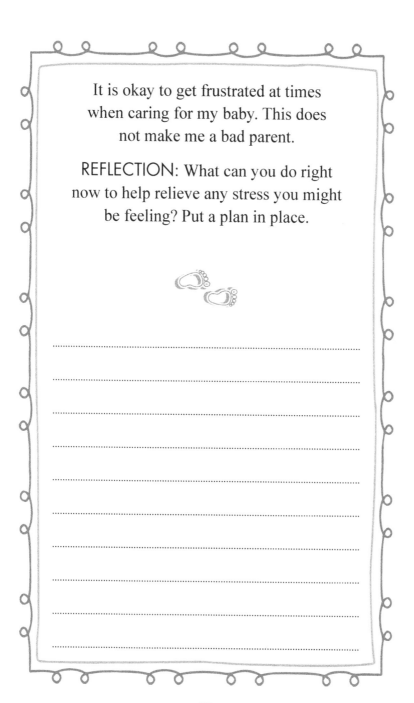

....

....

....

....

....

....

....

....

....

....

I resist the urge to plan out every moment, and instead, go with the flow.

REFLECTION: What is one thing you can stop stressing about today, and instead, just go with the flow?

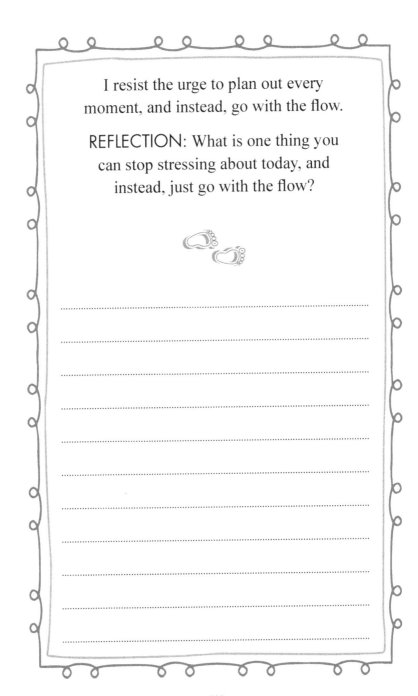

....

....

....

....

....

....

....

....

....

....

I do not have to remain in the darkness.

REFLECTION: What do you need clarity about today? Write it down and make a plan.

....

....

....

....

....

....

....

....

....

....

I release all thoughts that have raced through my mind all day and fall into a peaceful sleep.

REFLECTION: What is your bedtime routine?

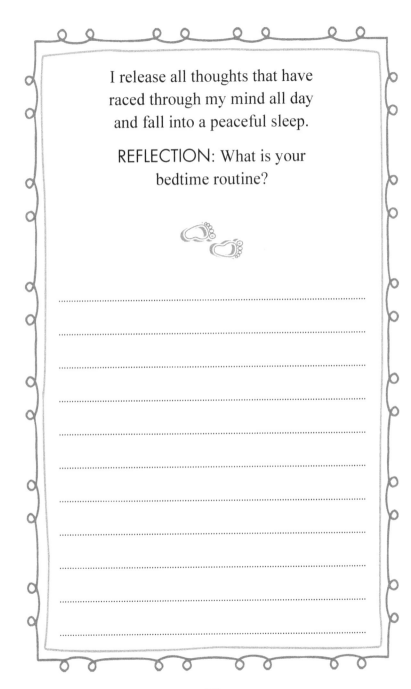

....

....

....

....

....

....

....

....

....

....

....

....

I accept that life is not perfect.

REFLECTION: What helps you to accept disappointments in life?

....

....

....

....

....

....

....

....

....

....

....

....

I am able to handle my baby's
temper tantrum.

REFLECTION: What tactic can you
use to help calm your baby down?

....

....

....

....

....

....

....

....

....

....

....

....

There is no room for anger in
my heart because I fill it up with
forgiveness and understanding.

REFLECTION: Write down one way that
you can show understanding to someone
with whom you have been angry.

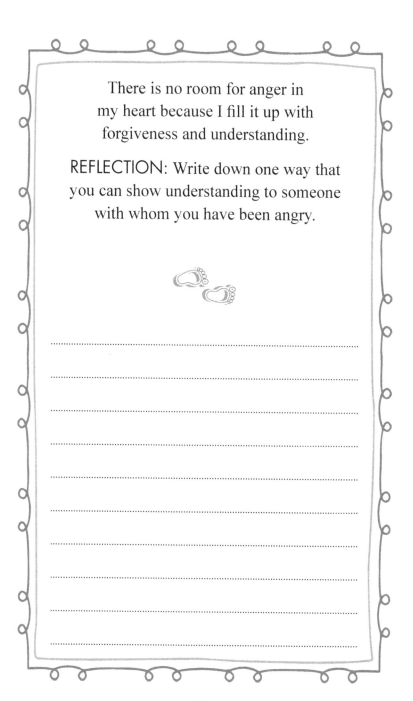

....

....

....

....

....

....

....

....

....

I let go of expectations and
work on the here and now.

REFLECTION: What is one way you
can focus on the here and now?

....

....

....

....

....

....

....

....

....

....

....

....

Setbacks and problems are part of life, but I am a problem-solver!

REFLECTION: Name a problem that you solved this week. Write it down.

....

....

....

....

....

....

....

....

....

....

....

It's never too late to start over.

REFLECTION: What do you need
to start afresh with today?

....

....

....

....

....

....

....

....

....

....

....

....

....

At times I feel isolated caring for my preemie at home, but I will do what it takes to keep my baby protected.

REFLECTION: If you have connected with other parents during your NICU stay who also now have preemies at home, reach out to them. If not, go online and join a support group for preemie parents after discharge.

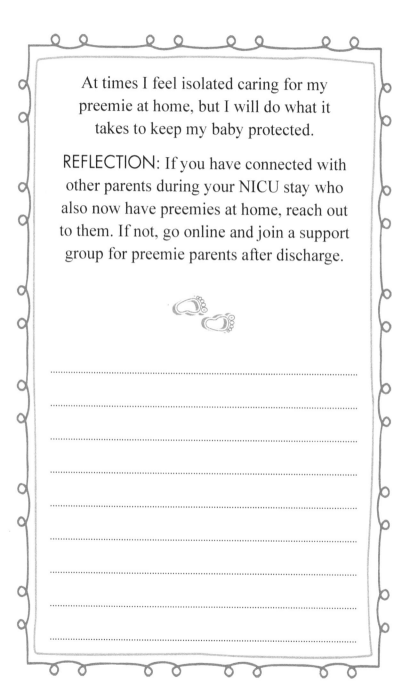

....

....

....

....

....

....

....

....

I have enough help at home to
do what must be done.

REFLECTION: Who helps you at home?

....

....

....

....

....

....

....

....

....

....

....

....

....

I don't raise my baby exactly like my parents raised me, and that's okay.

REFLECTION: Name one thing that you have made a conscious decision to do differently with your baby.

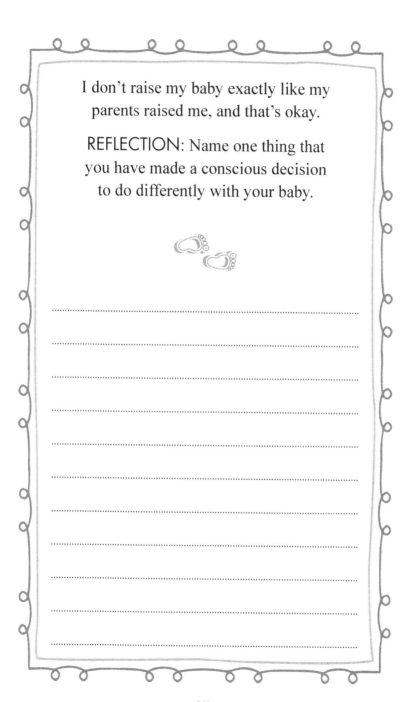

....

....

....

....

....

....

....

....

....

....

My partner and I work together to sacrifice whatever we have to in order to take care of our preemie.

REFLECTION: What do you appreciate most about your partner?

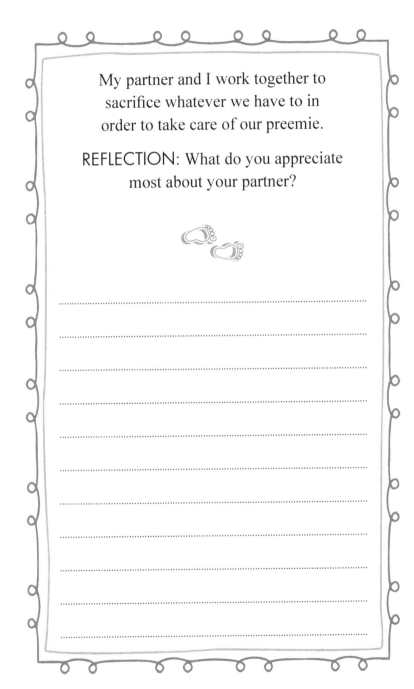

....

....

....

....

....

....

....

....

....

....

....

Seeking the approval of others will
not improve the quality of my life.

REFLECTION: Trust that you have
what you need to make the right
decisions for your preemie.

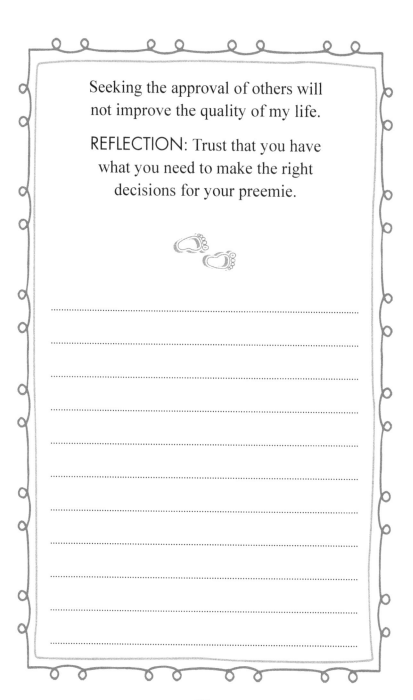

....

....

....

....

....

....

....

....

....

....

My baby is home now and things are
still hard, but we will get through it!

REFLECTION: Write down
one thing that has improved since
your baby made it home.

....

....

....

....

....

....

....

....

....

....

Watching my baby struggle to gain weight is heart-wrenching, but I believe that things will get better.

REFLECTION: Take some time to read about other preemies who have struggled to gain weight and feed but are now doing better.

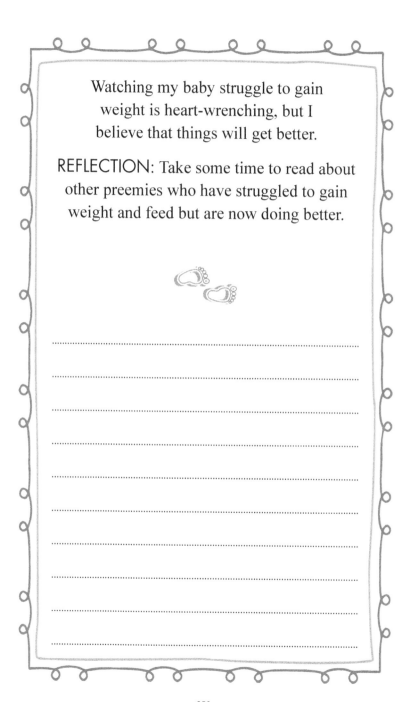

....

....

....

....

....

....

....

....

....

I can say no without feeling guilty.

REFLECTION: There are times when we all need to say no. What does saying no give you the freedom to do?

....

....

....

....

....

....

....

....

....

....

....

Life unfolds in the way that it should.

REFLECTION: How does that
make you feel?

....

....

....

....

....

....

....

....

....

....

....

I choose to be
a positive influence in this world,
and to touch someone's life today.

REFLECTION: What is one thing you can
do to make someone else's day better?

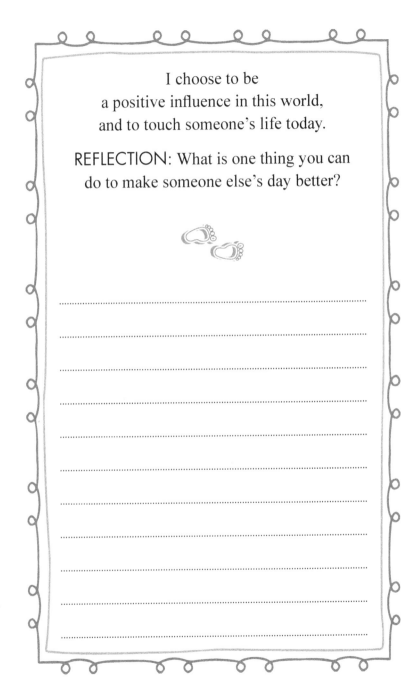

....

....

....

....

....

....

....

....

....

....

....

There are many things that demand
my attention, but I pause, stay
calm, and remain focused.

REFLECTION: Write down three things that
help you to balance life's responsibilities.

....

....

....

....

....

....

....

....

....

....

A failure is just another opportunity
to grow and stretch.

REFLECTION: Name one
failure that has given you an
opportunity to grow.

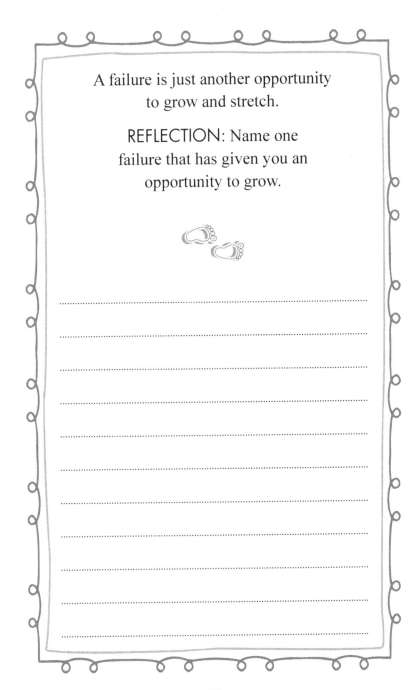

....

....

....

....

....

....

....

....

....

....

....

I have more and more energy every day.

REFLECTION: What are three things you can do to improve your energy?

....

....

....

....

....

....

....

....

....

....

Even if I don't feel it, I am amazing!

REFLECTION: Write down three positive attributes about yourself.

....

....

....

....

....

....

....

....

....

....

....

....

I am a warrior, and through God's grace, there is no battle I can't win.

REFLECTION: How has God been a source of strength for you during this difficult time?

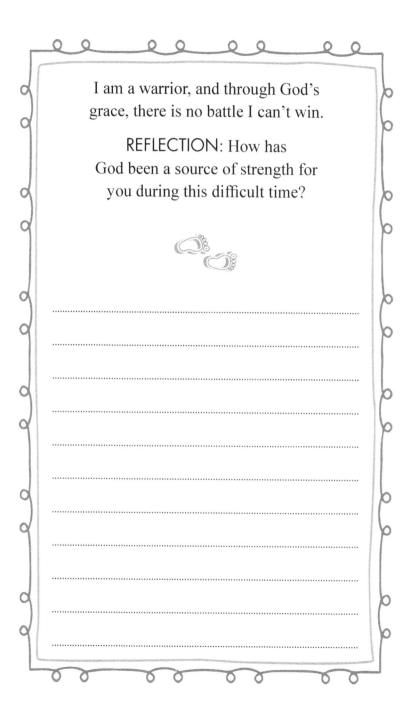

....

....

....

....

....

....

....

....

....

....

Nothing is impossible with God.

REFLECTION: Name one thing you thought was impossible that God proved you wrong about.

....

....

....

....

....

....

....

....

....

....

....

....

This is not the life I planned for my baby, but it is spectacular nonetheless!

REFLECTION: Name three ways in which you have learned to adapt to having a preemie.

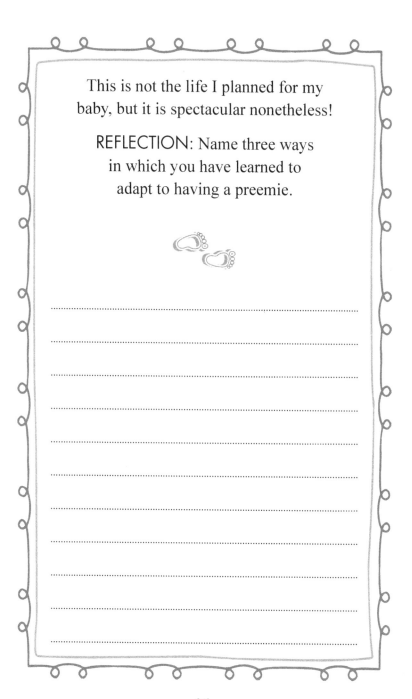

....

....

....

....

....

....

....

....

....

....

My baby has challenges but s/he is alive, and challenges are a part of life.

REFLECTION: What is the most important thing you want your baby to know about the world?

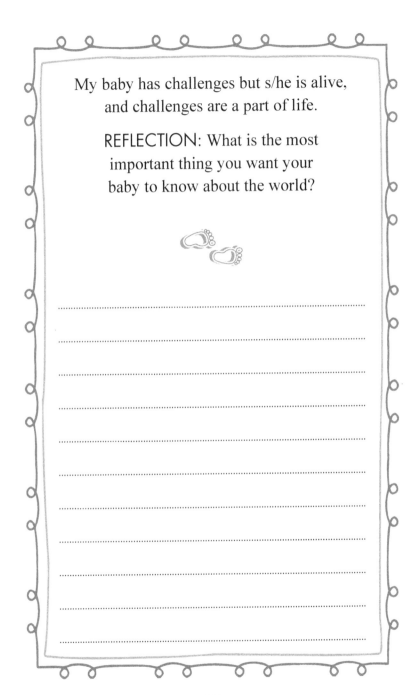

....

....

....

....

....

....

....

....

....

....

....

My baby is not bound by other people's expectations.

REFLECTION: Write down your baby's progress, and reflect on how far s/he has come.

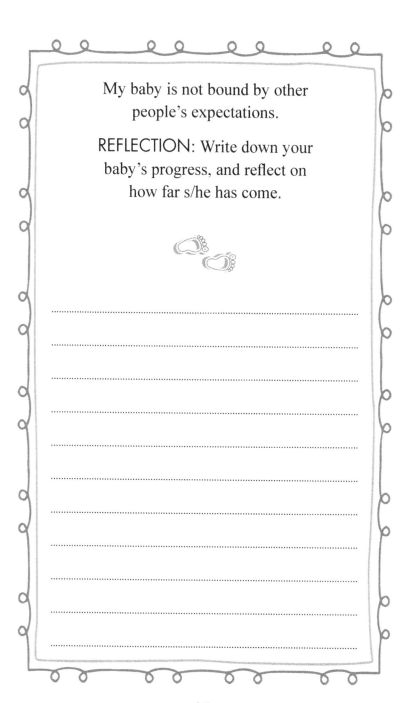

....

....

....

....

....

....

....

....

....

....

I believe my baby will have a good life.

REFLECTION: Now that you are home, what hopes do you have for your baby in the future? Write down two hopes for your baby's future.

....

....

....

....

....

....

....

....

....

....

My love for my baby is unshakeable.

REFLECTION: Who in your life shows you unshakeable love?

....

....

....

....

....

....

....

....

....

....

....

....

I am always growing and evolving.

REFLECTION: Change doesn't happen overnight. What helps you to remain consistent?

....

....

....

....

....

....

....

....

....

....

....

I do not let doubt rule my reality.

REFLECTION: What do you
do to alter your mindset?

....

....

....

....

....

....

....

....

....

....

....

Being at home is a new challenge but my preemie and I have what it takes.

REFLECTION: Name one challenge you have overcome since transitioning home.

....

....

....

....

....

....

....

....

....

....

....

....

I accept my circumstances and
resist the urge to complain.

REFLECTION: Write down three possible
solutions to a current challenge you face.

....

....

....

....

....

....

....

....

....

....

....

My history does not have to repeat itself.

REFLECTION: We gain
perspective from our experiences.
How has your history helped
prepare you for the future?

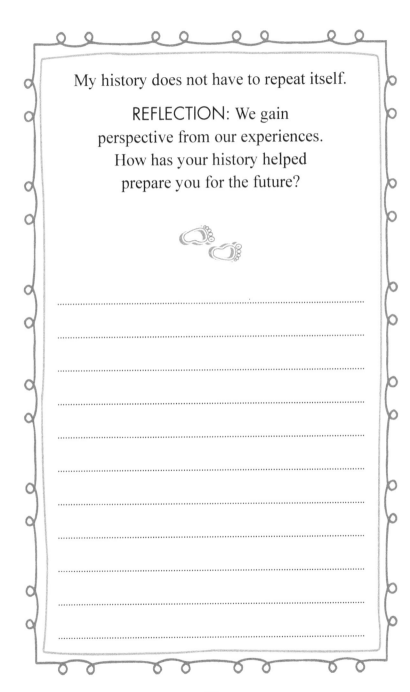

....

....

....

....

....

....

....

....

....

....

I pause, take a breath, and focus
on the good in my life.

REFLECTION: How often do
you pause for reflection?

....

....

....

....

....

....

....

....

....

....

....

....

My baby now makes eye contact, and
I feel more a part of her/his world.

REFLECTION: What other special things
do you share with your preemie?

....

....

....

....

....

....

....

....

....

....

....

All of my preemie's needs are being met.

REFLECTION: Who is helping to make sure your preemie is taken care of?

....

....

....

....

....

....

....

....

....

....

....

Experiencing intense stress and nightmares do not make me crazy, and I am not alone.

REFLECTION: Do you have someone you can share these experiences with? If not, find someone who can serve in this role.

....

....

....

....

....

....

....

....

....

....

Admitting that I need the help of a therapist makes me an even better mom.

REFLECTION: How has seeing a counselor to talk about your experiences made you feel?

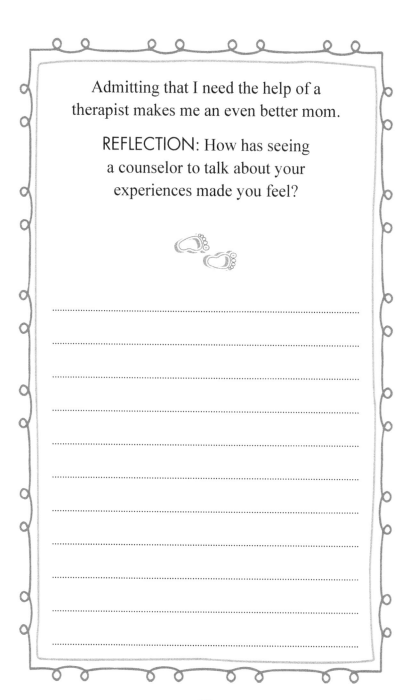

....

....

....

....

....

....

....

....

....

....

"Special needs" is just a label, and it
doesn't have to define my baby.

REFLECTION: How would you
explain who your baby is?

....

....

....

....

....

....

....

....

....

....

....

....

Disagreements between my partner and I don't mean that we don't love each other.

REFLECTION: When was the last time you had time for just the two of you? Take some time and plan a special night out.

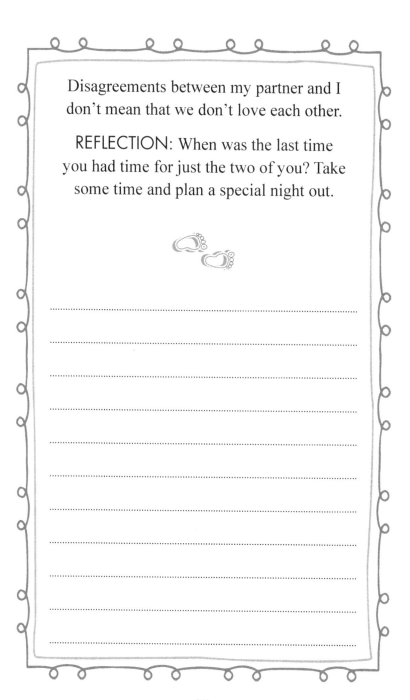

....

....

....

....

....

....

....

....

....

....

My baby needs special help, and
that doesn't mean that I'm a failure
as a mom, or that it is my fault.

REFLECTION: Are you part of a preemie
parent support group or blog? If you are,
find out what advice you can gain from
moms who have shared some of your same
experiences. If not, find one and join.

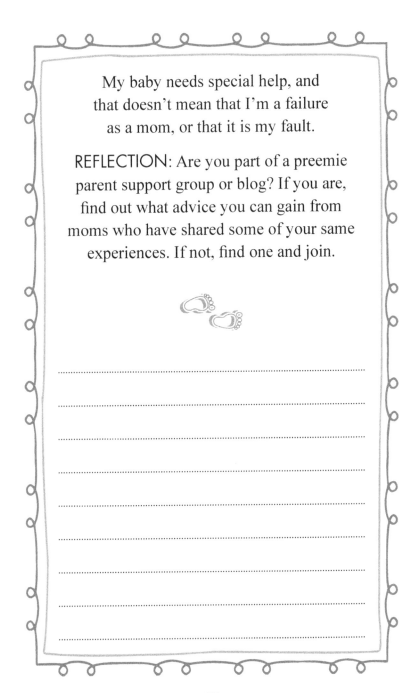

I am not alone!

REFLECTION: Who else is on this journey with you and your baby?

....

....

....

....

....

....

....

....

....

....

....

....

I will not be overcome with frustration
when others don't understand that
my baby may look normal but has
challenges that aren't readily apparent.

REFLECTION: Take a deep breath and count
to ten. Recognize that this misunderstanding
is a trigger for frustration and prepare a
response for moments like these in advance.

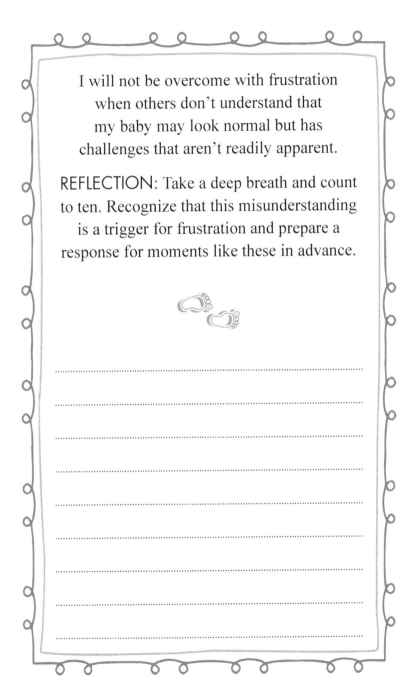

....

....

....

....

....

....

....

....

....

Everything that happened over this
past year has been for a purpose.

REFLECTION: What do you
think that purpose is?

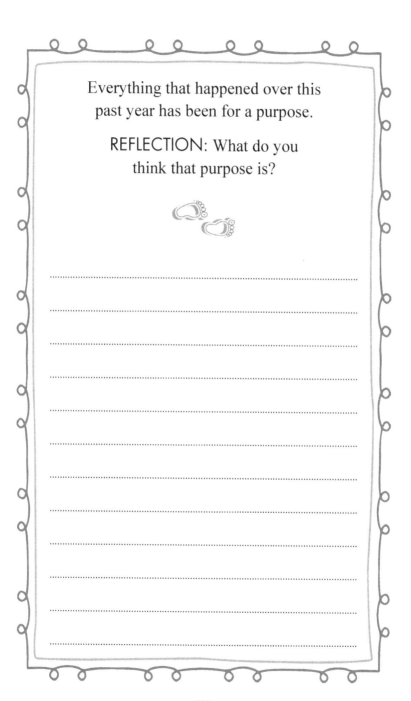

....

....

....

....

....

....

....

....

....

....

....

Home Affirmations

GOALS AND PROMISES

I focus on the things that bring me joy.

REFLECTION: What brings you great joy?

....

....

....

....

....

....

....

....

....

....

....

....

I am enthusiastic about the future!

REFLECTION: Write down three things you are looking forward to.

....

....

....

....

....

....

....

....

....

....

....

....

I have the power to inspire others.

REFLECTION: What are a few ways
you can inspire your baby?

....

....

....

....

....

....

....

....

....

....

....

Whatever is next, I am able to handle it.

REFLECTION: Where does
your strength come from?

....

....

....

....

....

....

....

....

....

....

....

My preemie will continue to thrive and grow.

REFLECTION: What goal did your
preemie achieve this week?

....

....

....

....

....

....

....

....

....

....

....

....

My family and I are making it through this journey, and we are a source of hope for all of those who come behind us!

REFLECTION: What is the most important thing you would want another family with a preemie at the beginning of her/his journey to know?

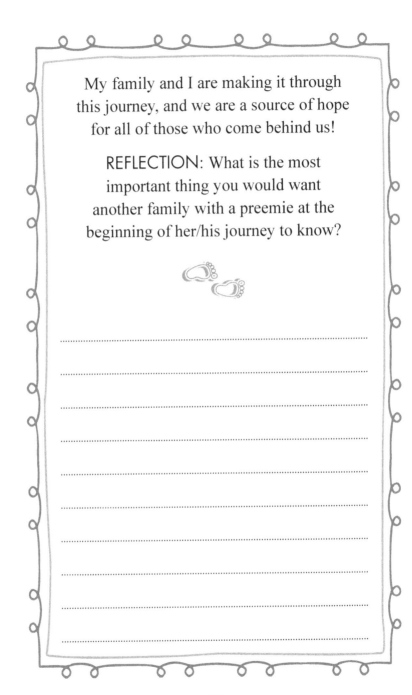

....

....

....

....

....

....

....

....

....

....

I give myself the permission to admit that I am not perfect and to accept that it's okay.

REFLECTION: Write down one thing that you love about yourself.

....

....

....

....

....

....

....

....

....

....

....

My family is destined for a life of abundance.

REFLECTION: In what ways are you experiencing abundance right now?

....

....

....

....

....

....

....

....

....

....

....

....

I make it a priority to live a life
not overburdened by worries.

REFLECTION: How can you
make this possible?

....

....

....

....

....

....

....

....

....

....

....

I wake up in the morning feeling refreshed and ready to face the day.

REFLECTION: What is your morning routine? How does it help you start off the day on a positive note?

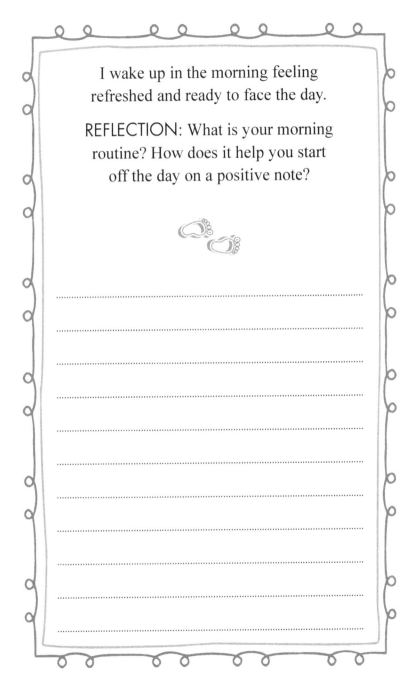

....

....

....

....

....

....

....

....

....

....

....

I must not only be kind to others; I also need to be kind to myself.

REFLECTION: What is one way you can be kind to yourself today?

....

....

....

....

....

....

....

....

....

....

I trust that good things will
happen for my family.

REFLECTION: Write down one wish
that you have for your family.

....

....

....

....

....

....

....

....

....

....

....

....

....

I must take time out for relaxation so that I can be there for my baby and my family.

REFLECTION: What can you do to take some time for yourself today?

....

....

....

....

....

....

....

....

....

....

....

I radiate confidence in all that I do.

REFLECTION: What uncompleted action can your confidence help you accomplish?

....

....

....

....

....

....

....

....

....

....

....

....

....

....

I am excellent at finding solutions to challenges that my baby faces.

REFLECTION: What are some challenges you helped resolve for your baby?

....

....

....

....

....

....

....

....

....

....

I will never give up on my baby.

REFLECTION: What helps
you to keep going?

....

....

....

....

....

....

....

....

....

....

....

....

I will do whatever it takes so that my baby has all s/he needs to continue to blossom.

REFLECTION: How is your baby changing/blossoming?

....

....

....

....

....

....

....

....

....

....

....

It is important for my baby not only to feel loved, but also heard and understood.

REFLECTION: How do you show your baby that s/he is special to you?

....

....

....

....

....

....

....

....

....

....

....

....

Today I forgive myself and accept
that I am worthy of love.

REFLECTION: Write down at least one
reason why you deserve to be loved.

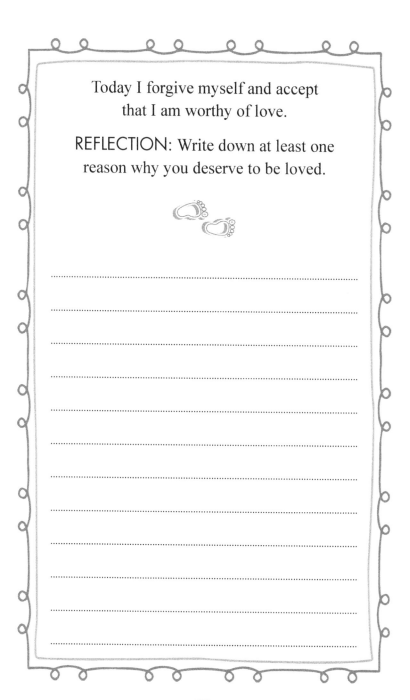

....

....

....

....

....

....

....

....

....

....

....

I have the power to change my thoughts.

REFLECTION: Write down five
uplifting things to meditate on.

....

....

....

....

....

....

....

....

....

....

....

....

This failure today is not the end; my preemie's journey continues.

REFLECTION: Say a prayer for your preemie right now.

....

....

....

....

....

....

....

....

....

....

....

Each trial I face builds my endurance.

REFLECTION: What insight have you gained from your most recent trial?

....

....

....

....

....

....

....

....

....

....

....

....

I let go of all grudges and instead,
maintain a mindset of peace and calm.

REFLECTION: Is there someone
that you need to forgive today?

....

....

....

....

....

....

....

....

....

....

....

I will not give up because there
is always another way!

REFLECTION: What solution can you find
today for a problem you are having?

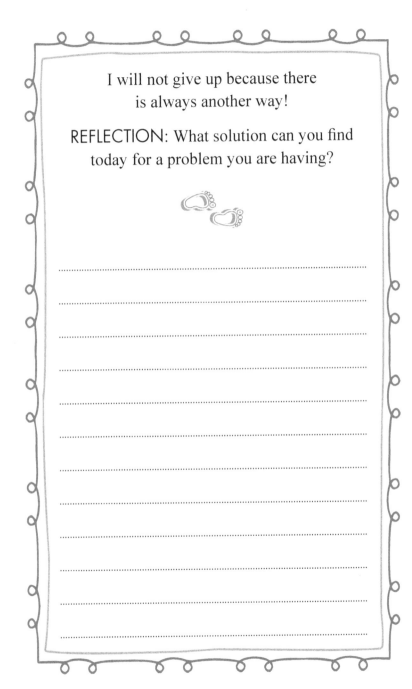

....

....

....

....

....

....

....

....

....

....

....

I will not compare my baby to others, but instead, proudly cheer on each step of progress s/he makes.

REFLECTION: Preemies develop at a different pace than term babies. Make an individualized chart for your baby, and every time s/he achieves a milestone, place a special marker.

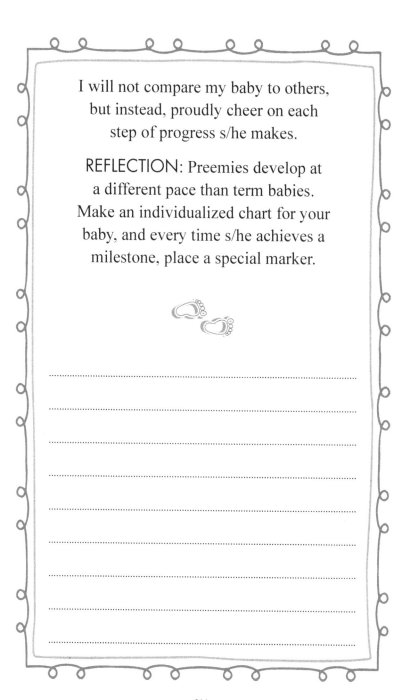

....

....

....

....

....

....

....

....

Exercise leads to improvement in
my physical and mental health.

REFLECTION: What is your favorite
exercise? Make some time do to it today.

....

....

....

....

....

....

....

....

....

....

....

....

My baby deserves the best!

REFLECTION: What one thing do
you want for your baby today?

....

....

....

....

....

....

....

....

....

....

....

Today was not a good day, but I
can find the silver lining!

REFLECTION: What is one thing
you can be glad about today?

....

....

....

....

....

....

....

....

....

....

....

....

Everyone needs forgiveness, and
today, I am starting with myself.

REFLECTION: Write down one thing
to forgive yourself for today.

....

....

....

....

....

....

....

....

....

....

....

No setback can keep me down!

REFLECTION: Name one thing you can do right now to improve how you feel.

....

....

....

....

....

....

....

....

....

....

....

....

Current circumstances do not
have to determine my reality.

REFLECTION: What change can you
make today to improve your future?

....

....

....

....

....

....

....

....

....

....

....

I eat a healthy, balanced diet most days.

REFLECTION: What can you do to make sure you are eating healthily?

....

....

....

....

....

....

....

....

....

....

....

I have what it takes to keep
my family together.

REFLECTION: What do you do to make
sure everyone in your family is cared for?

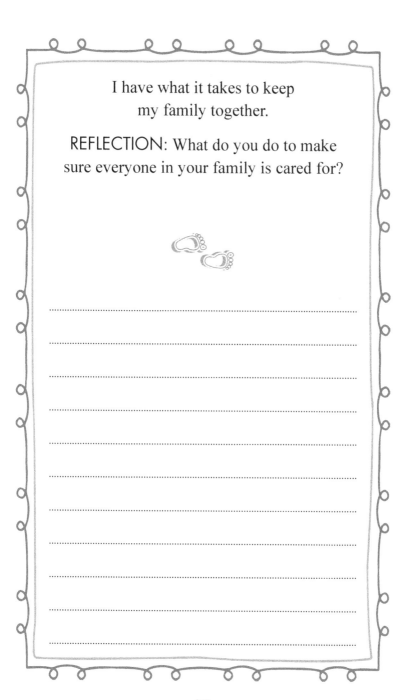

....

....

....

....

....

....

....

....

....

....

I will stop trying to predict the future, and instead, savor the present moment at hand.

REFLECTION: Write down one way that you can live in the moment today.

....

....

....

....

....

....

....

....

....

....

....

....

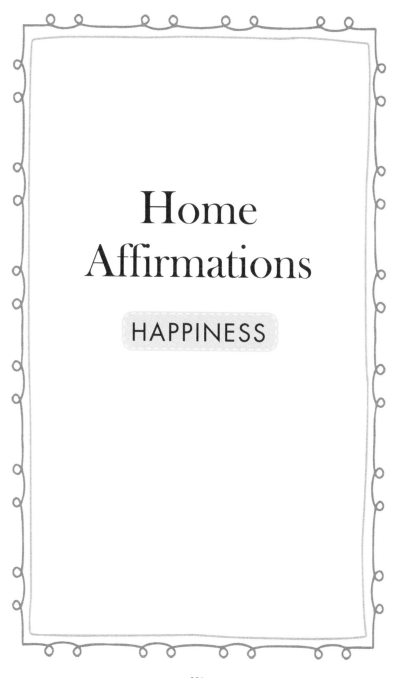

Home
Affirmations

HAPPINESS

Hearing my baby cooing is
like music to my ears.

REFLECTION: When did your
baby first start to coo?

....

....

....

....

....

....

....

....

....

....

Today will be a great day, and I
will celebrate each moment.

REFLECTION: Name one reason
to celebrate your preemie.

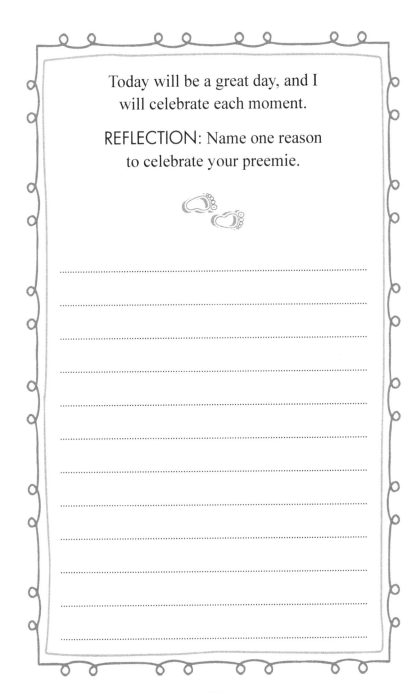

....
....
....
....
....
....
....
....
....
....
....
....
....

My baby is amazing and makes
me proud every day!

REFLECTION: Name one new
thing about your baby today.

....

....

....

....

....

....

....

....

....

....

....

Positivity is a habit.

REFLECTION: What have you been
doing to keep a positive spirit?

....

....

....

....

....

....

....

....

....

....

....

Behind every preemie is a great mommy
who loves and supports her/him!

REFLECTION: You are doing an amazing job,
Mom! Take a moment to acknowledge that!

....

....

....

....

....

....

....

....

....

....

....

....

No obstacle can stop my preemie's fight!

REFLECTION: Write down three wins your preemie has experienced so far.

....

....

....

....

....

....

....

....

....

....

Today will be a good day, and great things will come my way.

REFLECTION: Recall one good thing about your day today and write it down.

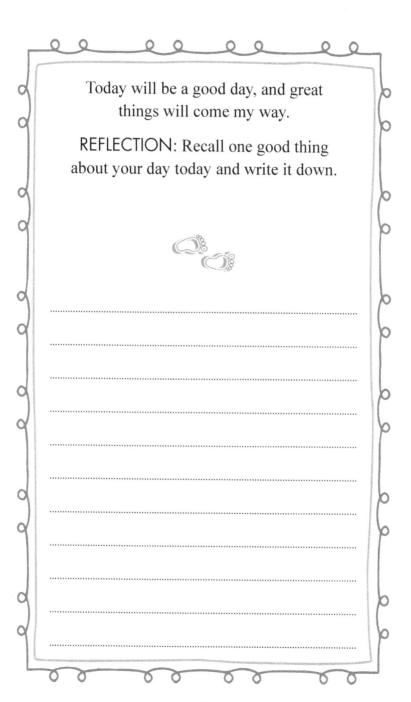

....

....

....

....

....

....

....

....

....

Every New Year is filled with
new possibilities!

REFLECTION: What is one wish you have
for your preemie for the upcoming year?

....

....

....

....

....

....

....

....

....

....

My preemie has so much love and support from people cheering her/him on!

REFLECTION: Who is a part of your preemie's village? Record each name for your preemie's memory book.

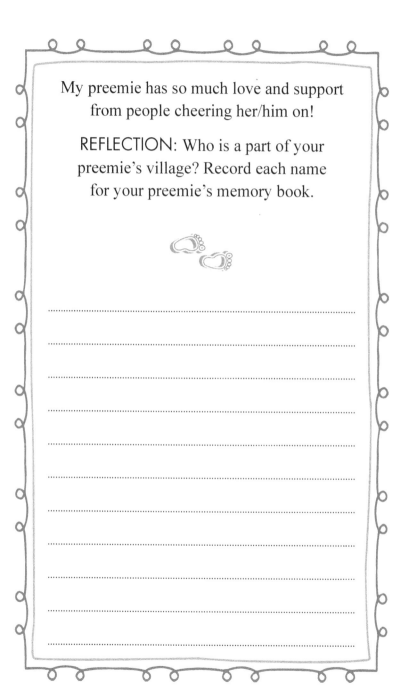

....

....

....

....

....

....

....

....

....

....

My baby has an excellent team
on the case: Mom and Dad!

REFLECTION: Name one way you and Dad
have been an excellent team for your baby.

....

....

....

....

....

....

....

....

....

....

....

....

I create an atmosphere of happiness
and warmth everywhere I go.

REFLECTION: Write down three things
to help you maintain a positive attitude.

....

....

....

....

....

....

....

....

....

....

....

No cloud in the sky can darken
the sunshine in my heart.

REFLECTION: Write down one thing
that keep the sun shining in your heart.

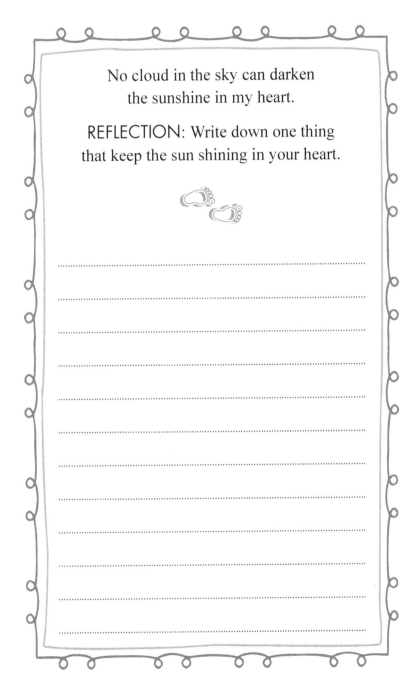

....

....

....

....

....

....

....

....

....

....

....

....

Having my family all together at home
is the best feeling in the world!

REFLECTION: Write down what it means
to you for all of you to finally be together.

....

....

....

....

....

....

....

....

....

....

....

I radiate peace and love to everyone I meet.

REFLECTION: How do you make
other people feel loved?

....

....

....

....

....

....

....

....

....

....

....

I walk with purpose.

REFLECTION: What is your purpose for this day?

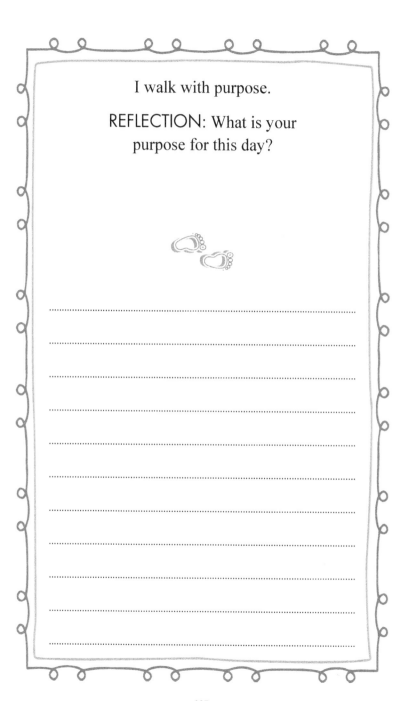

....

....

....

....

....

....

....

....

....

I can find the beauty in every situation,
if I only take the time to look.

REFLECTION: Name one thing of
beauty you have seen today.

....

....

....

....

....

....

....

....

....

....

....

In the quiet moments, I spend time holding my preemie close. No negative thoughts can intrude during these special times.

REFLECTION: What do you think about in those moments?

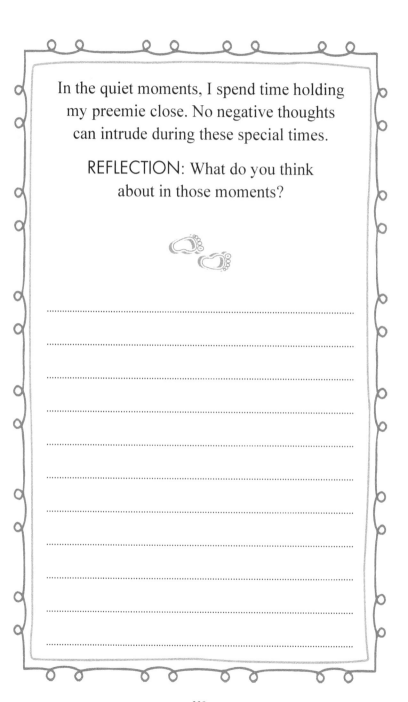

....

....

....

....

....

....

....

....

....

....

Today and every day I am filled with serenity.

REFLECTION: Write down five things
that help you to remain at peace.

....

....

....

....

....

....

....

....

....

....

....

....

I am beautiful on the inside and out.

REFLECTION: Write down three things that help you to remain beautiful on the inside.

....

....

....

....

....

....

....

....

....

....

....

Things can change for the better in an instant!

REFLECTION: Name one thing
that has changed for the better for
your baby in the past week?

....

....

....

....

....

....

....

....

....

....

....

....

Today will be an even better
day than yesterday!

REFLECTION: Write down one thing you can
do better today than you did the day before.

....

....

....

....

....

....

....

....

....

....

....

I focus on the joy in my surroundings.

REFLECTION: Write down three
things that bring you joy.

....

....

....

....

....

....

....

....

....

....

....

....

I am not perfect, but I am perfectly made.

REFLECTION: Write down one way you can show yourself some love today.

....

....

....

....

....

....

....

....

....

....

....

I take a deep breath and release the tension in my shoulders. Today will be a great day!

REFLECTION: Positive thoughts can improve your life. Plan now to take five minutes each day to focus on something positive before you start your day.

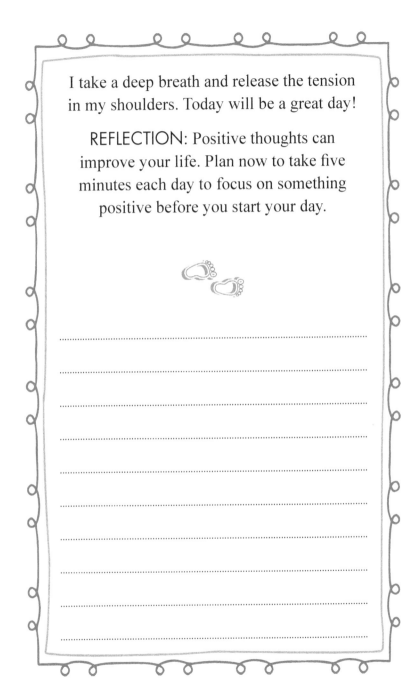

....

....

....

....

....

....

....

....

....

At times I thought we wouldn't make it, but we are here!

REFLECTION: Name another situation in your life you thought was impossible to manage. Write down how you made it through.

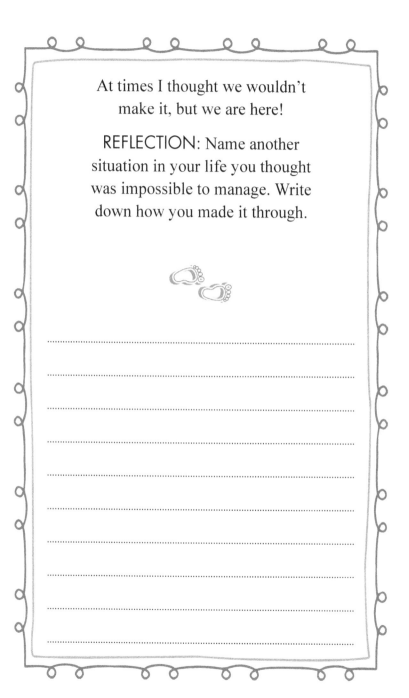

....

....

....

....

....

....

....

....

....

I am a compassionate and loving person.

REFLECTION: Write down the
name of someone that you can
show compassion to today.

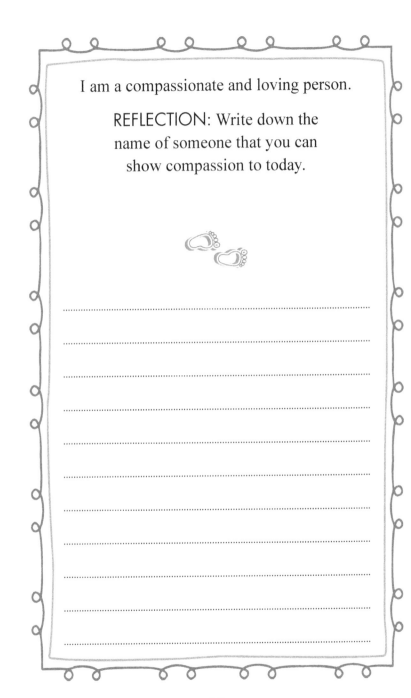

....

....

....

....

....

....

....

....

....

....

....

I work hard to maintain a good
attitude during this experience.

REFLECTION: Name a positive characteristic
that you are developing or honing through
this journey, and think of ways you can
share it with your preemie down the road.

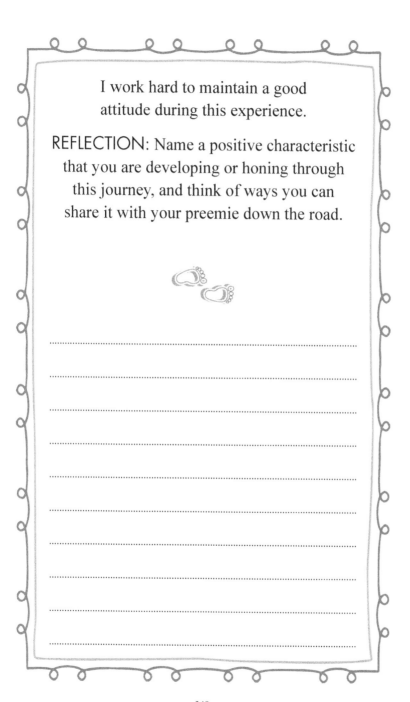

....

....

....

....

....

....

....

....

....

When my family spends quality
time together I feel tranquility.

REFLECTION: What is your favorite
thing to do with your family?

....

....

....

....

....

....

....

....

....

....

....

....

Seeing my baby's smile brings me
the greatest joy in the world!

REFLECTION: Name one thing
that makes your baby smile.

....

....

....

....

....

....

....

....

....

....

....

....

I know my baby has trials to face,
but I am here fighting alongside her/
him every step of the way.

REFLECTIONS: Name one way
in which you are a fighter.

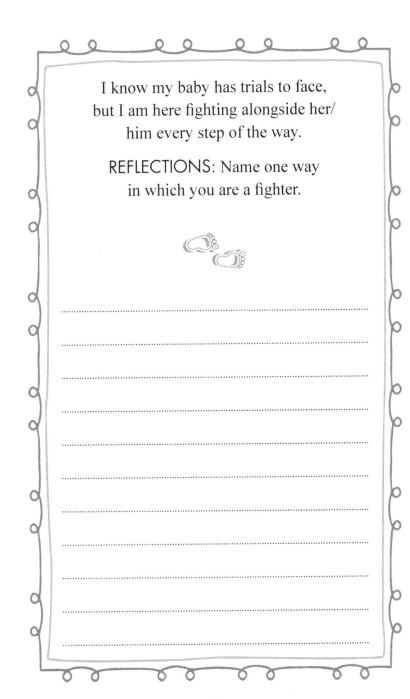

....

....

....

....

....

....

....

....

....

....

All of my family at home, together,
creates memories I will cherish forever.

REFLECTION: Create a family
collage and start a memory book.

....

....

....

....

....

....

....

....

....

....

....

....

At times my baby may struggle,
but s/he has a fighting spirit!

REFLECTION: Where does your baby
get this fighting spirit? Write it down.

....

....

....

....

....

....

....

....

....

....

....

My baby is full of wonderful surprises!

REFLECTION: Write down one wonderful surprise you noticed about your baby today.

....

....

....

....

....

....

....

....

....

....

....

....

Every day is a fresh new beginning.

REFLECTION: What new start
are you hoping for today?

....
....
....
....
....
....
....
....
....
....
....

All of the members of my family
are happy and content.

REFLECTION: Name three ways in
which your needs have been met.

....

....

....

....

....

....

....

....

....

....

I find pleasure in small victories.

REFLECTION: What small victory
have you achieved today?

....

....

....

....

....

....

....

....

....

....

....

Hearing my baby laugh lifts my spirits.

REFLECTION: What is one thing you can do to bring your baby joy today?

....

....

....

....

....

....

....

....

....

....

....

Watching my baby play is a dream come true.

REFLECTION: What is the next
dream you have for your baby?

....

....

....

....

....

....

....

....

....

....

I will enjoy the present, and
not live in the past.

REFLECTION: Name some of the good things
that your baby is currently experiencing?

....

....

....

....

....

....

....

....

....

....

I take time to feed my soul,
as well as my body.

REFLECTION: Write down three things
you can do to feed your soul.

....

....

....

....

....

....

....

....

....

....

....

I provide harmony and balance
in my baby's life.

REFLECTION: What helps you
to provide unity at home?

....

....

....

....

....

....

....

....

....

....

....

Every day is a new day for
new opportunities!

REFLECTION: What opportunity
are you excited about today?

....

....

....

....

....

....

....

....

....

....

....

The skies above and the oceans beneath cannot hold the love that I have for my baby.

REFLECTION: Name one way that a family member or friend has shown you love this week.

....

....

....

....

....

....

....

....

....

....

My baby is an unpredictable joy in my life.

REFLECTION: Name one unpredictable thing your baby has done.

....
....
....
....
....
....
....
....
....
....
....
....
....

My baby's eyes are filled with sunshine that makes today bright!

REFLECTION: What activity will you do with your baby today?

....

....

....

....

....

....

....

....

....

....

....

....

My baby is like a tiny seed that just keeps growing and growing.

REFLECTION: What do you do to continue your baby's growth?

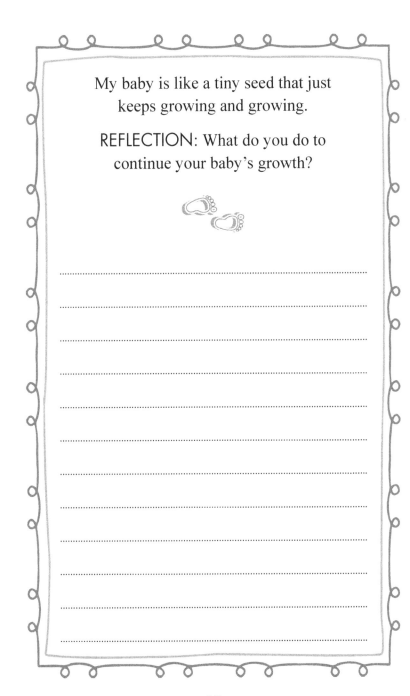

....

....

....

....

....

....

....

....

....

....

....

....

My baby marches to the beat of a different drum, and I love that.

REFLECTION: How do you embrace your baby's differences? What unique things can your baby provide to the world?

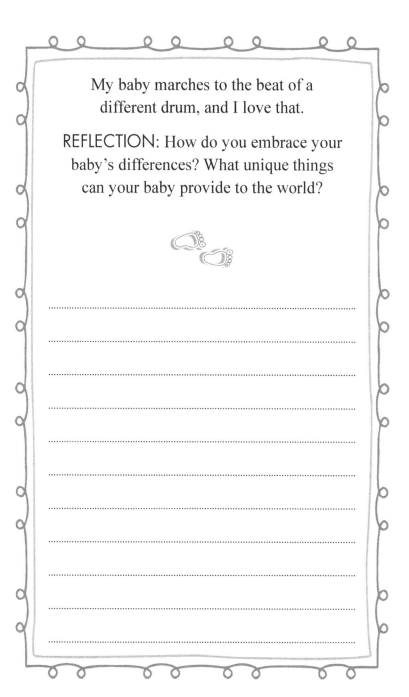

....

....

....

....

....

....

....

....

....

....

I choose to share my life with
people who bring me joy.

REFLECTION: Which individuals help you
to enjoy life? Call them up and say thanks.

....

....

....

....

....

....

....

....

....

....

....

....

My family is healthy and whole.

REFLECTION: What helps you to keep your family grounded?

....

....

....

....

....

....

....

....

....

....

....

My baby deserves all the good
the world has to offer.

REFLECTION: Name one way that
you provide for your baby.

....

....

....

....

....

....

....

....

....

....

....

....

Watching my baby sit up for the first time made me feel so proud!

REFLECTION: Name another milestone that you will be excited about when your baby achieves it?

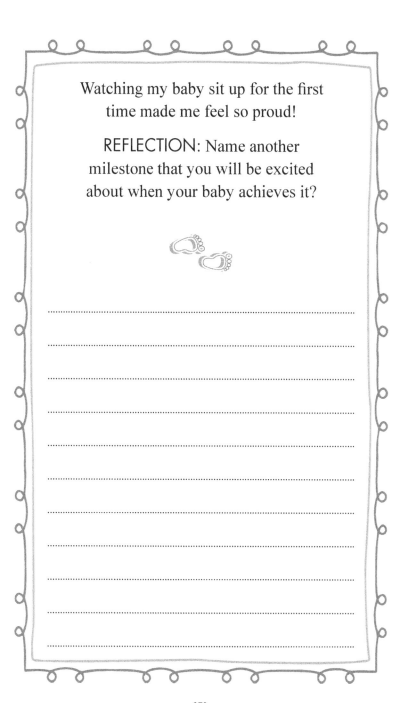

....

....

....

....

....

....

....

....

....

....

....

I have everything I need to be an
awesome mom for this baby.

REFLECTION: Write down
three of your strengths.

....

....

....

....

....

....

....

....

....

....

....

....

My baby is happy and treasured, and therefore, I am doing this job right.

REFLECTION: What else are you getting right in your life?

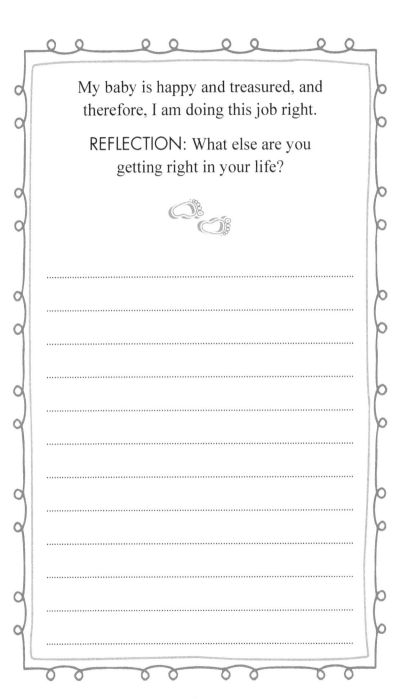

....

....

....

....

....

....

....

....

....

....

....

I deserve to be happy.

REFLECTION: What brings you happiness?

....

....

....

....

....

....

....

....

....

....

....

....

My baby loves to learn new things,
and I love to teach her/him.

REFLECTION: How have you been
a good teacher for your baby?

....

....

....

....

....

....

....

....

....

....

....

....

I shower my little one with praises to encourage her/him along the way as s/he learns.

REFLECTION: What are some encouraging words that you say?

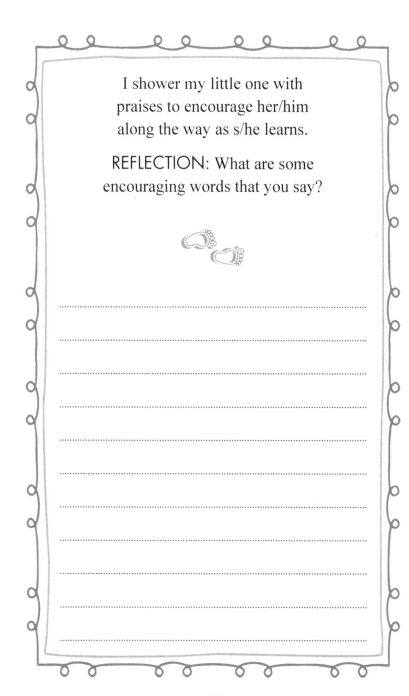

....

....

....

....

....

....

....

....

....

....

I enjoy the fact that, more and more, I am starting to see my baby's personality.

REFLECTION: Do any traits remind you of yourself? What about your partner?

....

....

....

....

....

....

....

....

....

....

....

....

I learned how to be the best mom from the awesome example I had in my mother.

REFLECTION: What is the greatest lesson you learned from your mom?

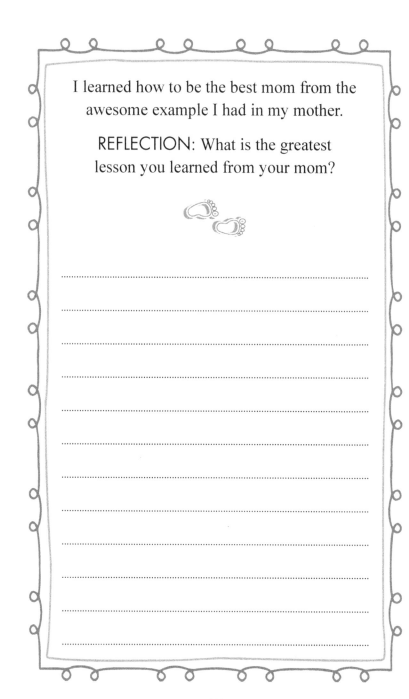

....

....

....

....

....

....

....

....

....

....

....

....

I love and accept my baby just as s/he is.

REFLECTION: What can you do
to let your baby know you don't
expect her/him to be perfect?

....

....

....

....

....

....

....

....

....

....

....

Seeing my baby try so hard to improve
every day fills me with pride.

REFLECTION: What can you do
to let your baby know you see
how hard s/he is working?

....

....

....

....

....

....

....

....

....

....

Any time I'm around my baby it
immediately improves my day.

REFLECTION: How do you make
the most of each moment you have
to spend with your baby?

....

....

....

....

....

....

....

....

....

....

I am rich because I have my
family all around me.

REFLECTION: Why is your
family important to you?

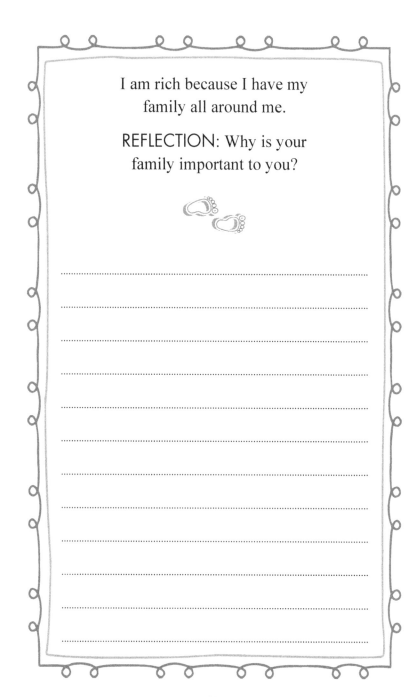

....

....

....

....

....

....

....

....

....

....

....

I embrace life and all that it has to offer.

REFLECTION: What is one pleasure
in life that you enjoy?

....

....

....

....

....

....

....

....

....

....

....

I am a loving and caring person, and I am setting a good example for my baby.

REFLECTION: What kind of person do you want your baby to be? List only the qualities that matter.

....

....

....

....

....

....

....

....

....

....

I am an excellent mother and partner!

REFLECTION: Name one nice thing you can do for your baby and partner today.

....

....

....

....

....

....

....

....

....

....

....

I mirror for my baby the good I
want to see in the world.

REFLECTION: What will you teach
your baby about relating to others?

....

....

....

....

....

....

....

....

....

....

....

The community for my preemie is
a tremendous group of individuals
filled with love and understanding.

REFLECTION: Who makes up
your baby's community?

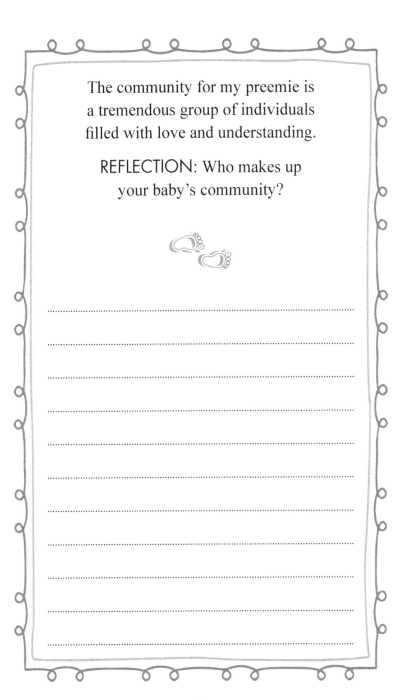

....

....

....

....

....

....

....

....

....

....

As my baby goes out into the world, I have confidence that the community will see the same beautiful baby that I do.

REFLECTION: How do you want others to view your baby?

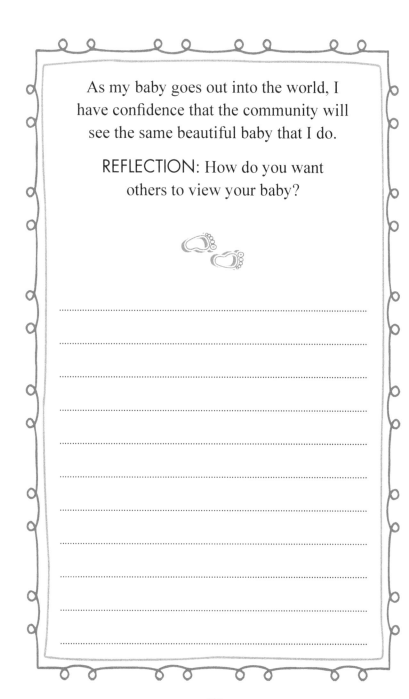

....

....

....

....

....

....

....

....

....

....

....

There is no better person than
my partner with whom I can
continue to go on this journey.

REFLECTION: Have you told your partner
how much you love and appreciate her/him?

....

....

....

....

....

....

....

....

....

....

....

Watching my baby learn new things
every day warms my heart.

REFLECTION: What is the newest
thing your baby has learned?

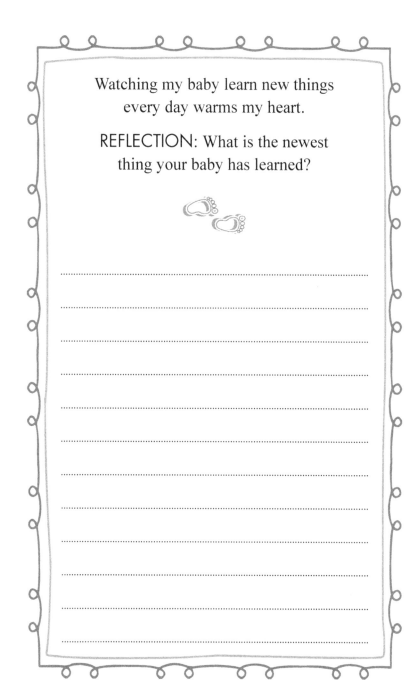

....

....

....

....

....

....

....

....

....

....

....

....

Nothing in this world will break the
bond that I have with my baby.

REFLECTION: Make sure to tell your
little one today that you love her/him.

....

....

....

....

....

....

....

....

....

....

....

Seeing my baby start to stand
is a great feeling!

REFLECTION: Add this milestone to your
memory book by writing down the date
and time the milestone was achieved.
You can also take a picture to include.

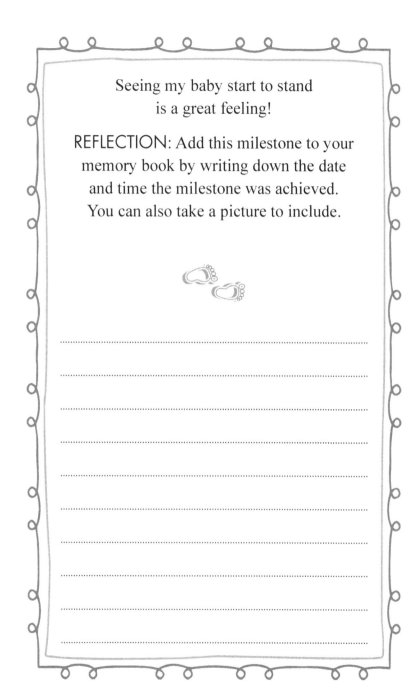

....

....

....

....

....

....

....

....

....

My baby's life is filled with abundance!

REFLECTION: In what ways does your baby have more than s/he needs?

....
....
....
....
....
....
....
....
....
....
....
....

My baby's first birthday is almost
here and s/he is a miracle!

REFLECTION: What was the most
amazing part of this journey?

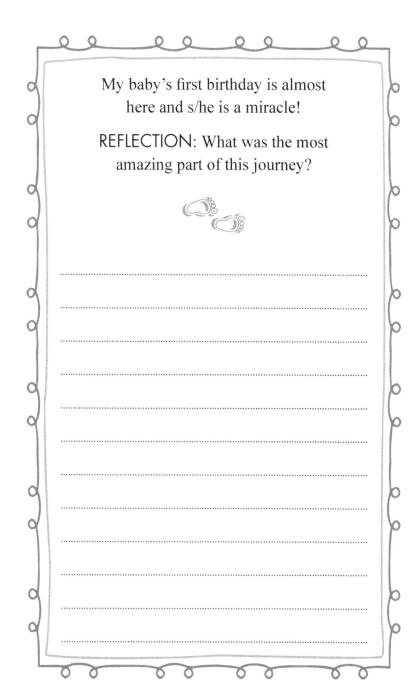

....

....

....

....

....

....

....

....

....

....

....

Now that you have completed this year of affirmations, please remember this final one: I love myself; therefore, I can truly love my baby!

REFLECTION: Write down two things that demonstrate self-love that will also be beneficial for your baby.

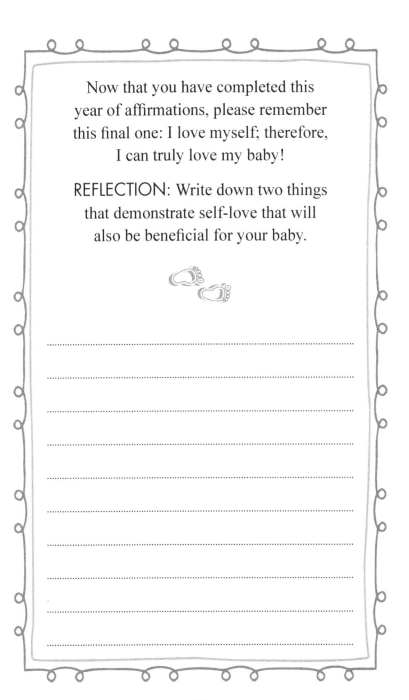

....

....

....

....

....

....

....

....

....

....

About the Author

Dr. Launice Melbourne is an author, speaker, social media expert, and board-certified pediatrician who specializes in neonatology. She graduated from medical school at Ohio State University, and is currently an attending physician at Virginia Hospital Center and Children's National Health Systems. Her mission in life is to care for sick infants and help the moms of these infants successfully transition into and out of life in the NICU.

Dr. Melbourne currently resides in Washington, D.C. When not providing medical care, she enjoys traveling, singing, writing poetry, and serving her community.

To connect, visit her website at www.drlaunicemd.com

CREATING DISTINCTIVE BOOKS
WITH INTENTIONAL RESULTS

We're a collaborative group of creative masterminds with a mission to produce high-quality books to position you for monumental success in the marketplace.

Our professional team of writers, editors, designers, and marketing strategists work closely together to ensure that every detail of your book is a clear representation of the message in your writing.

Want to know more?
Write to us at info@publishyourgift.com
or call (888) 949-6228

Discover great books, exclusive offers, and more at
www.PublishYourGift.com

Connect with us on social media

@publishyourgift